THE U.S. INDIVIDUAL INCOME TAX IS INCOMPATIBLE

WITH A

FREE SOCIETY

A Legal Justification for the Abolishment of the IRS and Replacement of the Income Tax with a National Sales Tax

ROBERT G. BEARD, JR.

ISBN: 978-1-4834-0249-9 (sc)
ISBN: 978-1-4834-0248-2 (e)
ISBN: 978-1-4834-0297-0 (e)

Because of the dynamic nature of the Internet, any web addresses or links contained in this book may have changed since publication and may no longer be valid.

The views expressed in this work are solely those of the author and do not necessarily reflect the views of the publisher, and the publisher hereby disclaims any responsibility for them.

Any people depicted in stock imagery provided by Thinkstock are models, and such images are being used for illustrative purposes only. Certain stock imagery © Thinkstock.

Lulu Publishing Services rev. date: 8/1/2013

PREAMBLE

According to Charles Adams the real cause of the American Revolution can be traced back to the reasons immigrants came to America—they sought freedom from taxation as expressed by one Irishman writing back home to Ulster in 1720:

Tell all the poor folk of ye place that God has opened a door for their deliverance . . . all that a man works for is his own, and there are no revenue hounds [i.e. no IRS] to take it from us here; there is no one to take away yer Corn, yer Potatoes.

In addition to understanding that many immigrants fled Europe because of oppressive taxation, along with the fact that they were also tax evaders and rebels themselves, our Founders read baron de Montesquieu's book, *The Spirit of Laws*, published in English in 1751, in which he set forth his basic principles of taxation: Direct taxes (e.g., tax on the wages of labor) were dangerous and natural to slavery; indirect taxes or taxes on the sale of merchandise were more natural to liberty.

Because of this belief that an income tax on a person's labor was tantamount to slavery, there was no peacetime income tax for the first 118 years of our existence. Then in 1894 Congress passed the first peacetime income tax that exempted 98% of the population; the tax rate was 2% on about 2% of the population; and, it was progressive because it exempted most of the population, representing *class legislation against the rich*. The Supreme Court got immediately involved in probably one of the most celebrated cases at the time and ultimately ruled the income tax unconstitutional.

However, after the adoption of the 16th Amendment in 1913 and as the nineteenth century came to a close, "the Court began abandoning its role as guardian of the Constitution so far as federal tax laws were concerned. As tax laws became increasingly abusive and even discriminatory, lacking even a semblance of uniformity, the Court washed its hands of them."

Because of the income tax laws, especially the administration and enforcement of them, individual freedom has been negatively impacted, while the Courts have either silently stood by or purposely let this happen.

This book is the publication of my Master of Laws (LL.M.) thesis, dated April 17, 2007. I graduated *Summa Cum Laude* on the 22nd of December 2008 from Thomas Jefferson School of Law, San Diego, California.

The purpose of this thesis is to point out that Congress, the IRS and the Judiciary, with the assistance of certain *academic enablers*, have perpetrated a fraud on the American people when it comes to the U.S. individual income tax. Four Supreme Court cases that were decided between 1886 and 1916 have been either (1) ignored, (2) misquoted, (3) misinterpreted, or (4) criticized without any rational basis that comports with the true meaning of the U.S. Constitution.

Many so-called *Constitutional Scholars* would like us to believe that the passage of the 16th Amendment, allowing Congress the ". . . power to lay and collect taxes on incomes, from whatever source derived . . . ," ended all legitimate challenges that the income tax is unconstitutional. I beg-to-differ and my thesis supports the following conclusions:

1. The U.S. individual income tax does not apply to most U.S. citizens or residents whose only income is from self-employment or salaries & wages. This is because a tax on the wages of labor represents a direct tax on property and a capitation tax; and, such taxes must be apportioned in accordance with the census. Since there is no apportionment requirement under existing law, this income is not gross income subject to tax for most U.S. citizens or residents.

2. The corporation income tax may be an excise tax for the privilege of doing business in corporate form and therefore, is not subject to apportionment. Accordingly, any net income from a regular corporation may be taxable under existing tax laws. But, issues still exist regarding the computation of taxable income. The term *taxes on incomes* included in the 16th Amendment has a specific meaning not subject to change without amendment. However, both Congress and the IRS continue to ignore the Constitution and continually change the definition of what is and is not *income* for tax purposes (see 4 below).

3. Under the original Constitution, which still exists today, *capitation and other direct taxes* include *a tax upon property holders in respect of their estates, whether real or personal, or of the income yielded by such estates.* Since such taxes are not currently required to be apportioned, most U.S. citizens and residents may not have any taxable income, except possibly, from the pass-through of any remaining "S" corporation earnings that have not been treated as salaries & wages. In spite of what you have read or heard, this is still the law, even though it has been ignored, misinterpreted, and intentionally forgotten.

4. Although Congress has the right to tax incomes, it must comply with all limitations set forth in the Constitution—they have not. The term *taxes on incomes* included in the 16th Amendment has a specific meaning, i.e. the meaning it had at the time of proposal and ratification. Therefore, Congress and the IRS have no right to continually change and redefine a Constitutional provision, which they have been doing for years.

5. In accordance with a Supreme Court decision in 1886, the U.S. individual income tax should be struck-down as unconstitutional since the law, as administered today, violates our rights under the 4th (the right to be secure in our papers and effects) and 5th (the right not to be compelled to be a witness against ourselves) Amendments to the U.S. Constitution.

6. By filing a Form 1040, U.S. Individual Income Tax Return, we waive our rights and privileges under the 5th Amendment and all the information provided in our tax returns can be used against us in a criminal proceeding. Since the civil and criminal penalties are unconscionable, a *Miranda* warning ought to be included with all instructions and requests for information by the IRS. In addition, Attorney's and C.P.A.'s, whose practices involve federal taxation, may be subject to malpractice claims if they do not advise their clients that they are waiving their constitutional rights by providing information to the IRS when audited; and, by signing and sending in tax returns under *penalties of perjury.*

The above conclusions are supported within this thesis. The 16th Amendment says Congress may tax incomes without apportionment but, it does not state that the 16th Amendment is superior to any other amendments and all other provisions of the Constitution. Therefore, Congress and the IRS have no authority to require U.S. citizens and residents to waive their rights under the Constitution, e.g., the 4th and 5th Amendments. But, this is exactly what is being done with respect to the administration and collection of U.S. income taxes. This is a fraud on the public.

Before this fraud becomes more readily understood by the populace at large, it would be prudent for Congress to: (1) Replace the U.S. individual income tax with a national sales or consumption tax; (2) get rid of the *Gestapo Tactics* of the IRS in forcing people to waive their rights; and (3) start the amendment process in Article V of the Constitution to abolish the 16th Amendment.

If Congress does not have the stomach to do the right thing, it is about time for practicing Attorney's and C.P.A.'s to step up and support their clients; and aggressively challenge the current thinking and propaganda spewed by Academia, Congress, the Judiciary, and the IRS.

Robert G. Beard, Jr., J.D., LL.M., C.P.A.

THE U.S. INDIVIDUAL INCOME TAX IS INCOMPATIBLE WITH A FREE SOCIETY

By

Robert G. Beard, Jr., JD, CPA
Candidate for the
LL.M. Degree in International Taxation
Walter H. & Dorothy B. Diamond Graduate
International Tax Program
St. Thomas University School of Law

Presented to

Professor William H. Byrnes, IV
Director and Founder,
Walter H. & Dorothy B. Diamond Graduate
International Tax Program
St. Thomas University School of Law
16400 NW 32nd Avenue
Miami, Florida 33054 U.S.A.

And

Professor Robert J. Munro
Thesis II
Walter H. & Dorothy B. Diamond Graduate
International Tax Program
St. Thomas University School of Law

April 17, 2007

TABLE OF CONTENTS

I. INTRODUCTION

For the past several years, the U.S. Internal Revenue Service (IRS) has released the "Dirty Dozen" notorious tax scams, which has included "Frivolous Arguments". Among other things, this category consists of the claim that wages are not taxable income; that filing a return and paying taxes are merely voluntary; and, the requirement to file Form 1040 violates the Fifth Amendment right against self-incrimination and the Fourth Amendment right to privacy. According to the IRS, such arguments are false and no one has a right to disobey the law.[1]

Today, the Courts, many scholars and lawyers, and, the average American tend to agree with the IRS that these arguments are indeed frivolous. However, there may very well be a reasonable basis for individual taxpayers to make these claims. For, as Senator Elihu Root stated during the debate on the first income tax act following the passage of the 16th Amendment, "... no one understands the Income Tax Law except persons who have not sufficient intelligence to understand the questions that arise under it."[2]

However, even though a reasonable basis may exist, in certain situations, for a U.S. Citizen or resident to not file an income tax return and to not pay taxes, it is highly unlikely that a Court

---

1 I.R.S. News Release, IR-2006-25, Feb. 7, 2006, http://www.irs.gov/newsroom/article/0,,id=154293,00.html and I.R.S. News Release, IR-2007-37, Feb. 20, 2007, http://www.irs.gov/newsroom/article/0,,id=167983,00.html.
2 Lowell H. Becraft, Jr., *Uncertainty of the Federal Income Tax Laws*, Sep. 1, 1999, http://home.hiwaay.net/~becraft/UNCERTAIN.html.

would ever rule in favor of such a position, thereby creating a fiscal disaster for the United States Government. Furthermore, to take such a position would most probably result in substantial legal fees; repayment of taxes, interest and penalties; and, may involve criminal charges with reliance on a jury to avoid imprisonment. In spite of what Chief Justice Warren said, "Our system of taxation is based upon voluntary assessment and payment, not upon distraint,"[3] today, failure to volunteer and pay your U.S. income taxes can be quite costly.

Professors Mazza and Kaye seem to agree that there may be constitutional problems or issues associated with the income tax laws today, "Upon close examination, many provisions of the U.S. Constitution could… restrict the legislative power to tax… Challenges, however, are rarely successful primarily because of the willingness of the courts to defer to the legislature on tax issues. This has led to the observation that there may be two Constitutions, one for taxes and one for all other matters."[4]

Accordingly, and assuming my analysis is deemed reasonable, the best that could be hoped for is that enough people become aware of the problems associated with the individual income tax as it relates to the Constitution; and, Congress is forced into doing the right thing, i.e., abolishing the individual income tax and replacing it with a national sales tax, a much more equitable approach to taxation in a free society. For, as it is hoped will be demonstrated in the following discussion, the U.S. individual income tax is incompatible with a free society.

---

3 Flora v. U.S., 362 U.S. 145, 641 (1960).

4 Stephen W. Mazza & Tracy A. Kaye, *Section IV: Constitutional and Administrative Law: Restricting the Legislative Power to Tax in the United States*, 54 Am. J. Comp. L. 641, 38, Fall 2006.

II. HISTORICAL BACKGROUND

America's Founders were tax rebels with history on their side. For well over a century, most of them believed that taxation "was nothing more than legalized robbery, a phrase they used repeatedly". "The wisdom of these men grew out of strife of the previous centuries. In England, a king had his head cut off over taxes. Under the strain of six major tax revolts, the great Spanish empire collapsed. Holland declined over too much tax, and in France, bloody tax revolts were everywhere."[5]

These great men understood the havoc bad taxation created and "searched through history for taxes that had worked and those that brought disaster". From the Greeks and Romans, they understood the relationship of taxes and tyranny; and, the relationship of taxes and prosperity. In addition, they learned from the British "how a supposedly good government, with noble constitutional principles, could adopt brutal, burdensome taxes, enforced by savage punishments".[6]

As far as the Founders were concerned, taxation was "…the root of most evil so far as civilized society was concerned, and they were determined, however naively, not to repeat European mistakes."[7]

---

5 Charles Adams, Those Dirty Rotten Taxes: The Tax Revolts that Built America, 16-18 (1998).

6 *Id.*

7 *Id.*

"A British scholar, writing about the founders, said that never in the course of history had there been so many men at one time and place so skilled in the art of statecraft. William Gladstone made a similar comment in 1887: The American Constitution is the most wonderful work ever struck off at a given time by the brain and purpose of man."[8]

With the creation of the Constitution, our Founders started a unique experiment in freedom for the individual; with limited government, funded by low indirect taxes; and, constitutional provisions to protect the individual from government and the tyranny of majority rule, i.e. democracy.

As far as democracy is concerned, in 1787 when Benjamin Franklin left the Constitutional Convention, a curious citizen asked what type of government they had established. Dr. Franklin's famous reply—"A Republic, if you can keep it."[9]

Whether we listen to the media, our elected officials, or the general public, all we seem to hear about is democracy and freedom; and, nothing about a republic. Furthermore, it appears that many people in the United States believe that the words democracy and freedom are interchangeable meaning one and the same. Nothing could be further from the truth… they are diametrically opposed terms. And, our Founders understood this.

Probably, the best illustration of a democracy is the example of two wolves and one sheep deciding what to have for dinner.[10] In other words, in a democracy the majority decides what the minority can or cannot do; and, what property the minority can keep, if any.

---

8 *Id.*
9 http://www.bartleby.com/73/1593.html.
10 Richard J. Maybury, Whatever Happened to Justice, 125 (1993).

James Madison, the architect of our Constitution, expressed his fear and concern as follows, "...democracies have ever been spectacles of turbulence and contentions; have ever been found incompatible with personal security or the rights of property; and have in general been as short in their lives as they have been violent in their death."[11] The Founders clearly understood the dangers inherent in a democracy and Edmund Randolph of Virginia probably best describes their efforts at the Constitutional Convention, "The general object was to produce a cure for the evils under which the United States labored; that in tracing these evils to their origins, every man had found it in the turbulence and follies of democracy." All the participants at the Convention shared the same views regarding the evils associated with democracy.[12]

The Founders believed that a democracy meant centralized power, controlled by majority opinion, which would become completely arbitrary, resulting in the continued age-old concept of the rule of man. Whereas, by establishing a republic, which was decentralized and representative in nature, with the government's purpose limited to protecting liberty and private property rights, the United States would enter the enlightened age of the rule of law.[13]

Accordingly, our Founders gave us a constitutional republic with written guarantees to protect individual freedom and property rights. The government created in 1787 is best described by Thomas Jefferson, "... a wise and frugal government, which shall restrain men from injuring one another, which shall leave them

---

11 The Federalist No. 10 (James Madison).
12 Ron Paul, M.D., Congressman, U.S. House of Representatives, *Sorry, Mr. Franklin, "We're All Democrats Now"*, Jan. 29, 2003, http://www.originalintent.org/commentaries/RonPaulonDemocracy.pdf.
13 *Id.*

otherwise free to regulate their own pursuits of industry and improvement, and shall not take from the mouth of labor the bread it has earned. This is the sum of good government, and this is necessary to close the circles of our felicities."[14]

As stated by Thomas Jefferson, the government they established did not contemplate a tax on income or wages, i.e. "… a wise and frugal government… shall not take from the mouth of labor the bread it has earned."[15]

---

14 Thomas Jefferson, First Inaugural Address, Mar. 4, 1801, http://www. cato.org/about/thomas.html.

15 *Id.*

III. TAXING POWER OF CONGRESS

A. Direct and Indirect Taxes

The taxing power of Congress is set forth in Article I, Section 8 of the Constitution—"The Congress shall have Power to lay and collect Taxes, Duties, Imposts and Excises..."[16] However, there are three limitations, the first is found in Section 8 while the remaining two are in Section 9: (1) "... all Duties, Imposts and Excises shall be uniform throughout the United States;"[17] (2) "No Tax or Duty shall be laid on Articles exported from any State;"[18] and, the limitation, which is most important for purposes of this discussion, (3) all Capitation and Direct Taxes must be apportioned.[19]

Accordingly, there are four types of taxes identified in the Constitution: (1) Taxes, which are considered direct taxes; (2) Duties; (3) Imposts; and, (4) Excises. At the time the Founders used these terms, taxes fell into two categories... direct and indirect. As explained by Justice Cooley, the term Taxes was used "in contradistinction to these levies [duties, imposts and excises]". Therefore, since duties, imposts and excises were indirect taxes, the Founders use of the term Taxes above in (1) meant Direct Taxes.[20]

---

16 U.S. Const. art I, § 8.

17 *Id.*

18 U.S. Const. art. I, § 9.

19 *Id.*

20 Thomas Cooley, The General Principles of Constitutional Law in the United States of America, 55, (reprint Feb. 2001) (1880).

Justice Cooley defines duties and imposts as "nearly synonymous" and states they are usually levied on the import or export of commodities; while excises are "laid upon the manufacturer, sale or consumption of commodities... and upon licenses to pursue certain occupations."[21]

These definitions agree with those found in the Oxford English Dictionary, which traces the historical use of words or terms.[22] It also defines Direct Taxes as "one levied immediately upon the persons who are to bear the burden, as opposed to indirect taxes levied upon commodities." Furthermore, "A Tax is called direct when it is immediately taken from property or labor; and indirect when it is taken from them by making their owners pay for liberty to use certain articles, or exercise certain privileges."[23] According to M. Cutler... "There is, perhaps, no item in the catalogue of our taxes which has been more unpopular than that which is called the direct tax." And, the primary direct taxes in Great Britain, prior to and at the time of our founding, were Income and Property Taxes.[24]

As explained by Professor Tribe, the distinction between direct and indirect taxes was extremely important:

> Because of the impractical apportionment requirement attaching to direct taxes, the fate of federal income taxation in the nineteenth century turned on the content the Supreme Court gave to the distinction between direct and indirect taxes. In Pollock v. Farmers' Loan & Trust Co., a majority of the Justices ruled that, insofar as the

---

21 *Id.*

22 Oxford English Dictionary, Vol. IV, 703 & Vol. XVII, 677, (2d ed.).

23 *Id.*

24 *Id.*

source of income is property, an income tax is a direct tax; and is therefore invalid unless apportioned.[25]

The Founders intent, as indicated above, was for the federal government to rely primarily on indirect taxes for its revenue; and, only resort to direct taxation for "dire emergencies such as war". For the first 75 years of our existence, this form of taxation worked fairly well. "During the War of 1812 and its aftermath, direct taxes on property were levied and apportioned among the states to help pay for the war's cost. After collection, they then expired."[26]

B. Income Taxes Ruled Unconstitutional

However, as a result of the Civil War things began to change. "America's first income tax was adopted in the Civil War... and... was repealed after the war ended." But, Congress again decided to adopt an income tax in 1894, which was immediately "attacked and challenged in the courts". "Within a year it was before the United States Supreme Court..."[27] The name of this case was Pollock v. Farmers' Loan and Trust Company (*Pollock*).

In *Pollock*, the majority held the tax to be unconstitutional since the income tax on real estate was determined to be a direct tax; and, in violation of the apportionment requirement of the Constitution. The Court ruled that because a tax on real estate would be a direct tax, then the income derived from the real estate would also have to be considered a direct tax.[28]

---

25 Laurence H. Tribe, American Constitutional Law, 843, 3d ed., Vol. 1 (2000).

26 Nelson Hultberg, Why We Must Abolish the Income Tax and the IRS, 4, AFR Publications (1996).

27 Charles Adams, For Good And Evil, 360 (1993).

28 Pollock v. Farmers' Loan & Trust Co., 157 U.S. 429, Reh'g, 158 U.S. 601 (1895).

Mr. Chief Justice Fuller delivered the majority opinion noting that,

> ...it is within judicial competency, by express provisions of the Constitution or by necessary inference and implication, to determine whether a given law of the United States is or is not made in pursuance of the Constitution, and to hold it valid or void accordingly; [and] that the doctrine that courts must close their eyes on the Constitution, and see only the law, would subvert the very foundation of all written constitutions.[29]

Just as important, at least for purposes of this discussion, Justice Fuller stated,

> But in arriving at any conclusion upon this point, we are at liberty to refer to the historical circumstances attending the framing and adoption of the Constitution as well as the entire frame and scheme of the instrument... We inquire, therefore, what, at the time the Constitution was framed and adopted, were recognized as direct taxes? What did those who framed and adopted it understand the terms to designate and include?[30]

Justice Fuller then proceeded to review the "historical circumstances" surrounding "the framing and adoption of the Constitution". He referred to James Madison who stated direct taxation should not be used but in "cases of absolute necessity"; and, to Alexander Hamilton, who wrote in Federalist No. 36, referring to the rule of apportionment, "By prescribing this rule... the door was shut to partiality or oppression, and the abuse

---

29 Pollock v. Farmers' Loan & Trust Co., 157 U.S. 429, 810 (1895).
30 *Id.* at 681.

of this power of taxation to have been provided against with guarded circumspection."[31]

He then continued with his analysis to determine what was considered a direct tax at the time of the framing. In 1794, Congressman Sedgwick, in a debate in the House of Representatives, stated that direct taxes included a capitation tax; taxes on land and on property; and, taxes on income.[32]

Justice Fuller referred to a publication in 1796 by Albert Gallatin who wrote, "The most generally received opinion, however, is, that by direct taxes in the Constitution, those are meant which are raised on the capital or revenue of the people; by indirect, such as are raised on their expense." He also stated that Adam Smith believed that a tax on real estate and income were direct taxes; and, referred to Alexander Hamilton's brief for the government in *Hylton v. United States*, which was decided in 1796.[33]

Hamilton argued successfully that a duty on carriages was an excise tax because it was so in a British Statute; and, that "it is fair to seek the meaning of terms in the statutory language of that country from which our jurisprudence is derived." Therefore, according to Justice Fuller, "If the question had related to an income tax [in the *Hylton* case], the reference would have been fatal, as such taxes have been always classed by the law of Great Britain as direct taxes."[34]

Justice Fuller concluded his majority opinion with the following remarks:

---

31 *Id.* at 683 & 564.
32 *Id.* at 815.
33 *Id.* at 570 & 572.
34 *Id.* at 572.

If it be true that by varying the form the substance may be changed, it is not easy to see that anything would remain of the limitations of the Constitution, or of the rule of taxation and representation, so carefully recognized and guarded in favor of the citizens of each State. But constitutional provisions cannot be thus evaded. It is the substance and not the form which controls, as has indeed been established by repeated decisions of this court.

Nothing can be clearer than what the Constitution intended to guard against was the exercise by the general government of the power of directly taxing persons and property within any State through a majority made up from the other States...and was manifestly designed to operate to restrain the exercise of the power of direct taxation to extraordinary emergencies, and to prevent an attack upon accumulated property by mere force of numbers.[35]

Ending his discussion on this particular subject, Justice Fuller wrote,

If, by calling a tax indirect when it is essentially direct, the rule of protection could be frittered away, one of the great landmarks defining the boundary between the Nation and the States of which it is composed, would have disappeared, and with it one of the bulwarks of private rights and private property. We are of opinion that the law in question, so far as it levies a tax on the rents or income of real estate, is in violation of the Constitution, and is invalid.[36]

---

35 *Id.* at 581 & 820.
36 *Id.* at 583.

Since this was such a significant case, Justice Field also placed his opinion on the record: "Some decisions of this court have qualified or thrown doubts upon the exact meaning of the words direct taxes." Furthermore, "...on the subject of direct taxes in the British Parliament an income tax has been...designated as a direct tax..." In addition, "There is no such thing in the theory of our national government as unlimited power of taxation in Congress."[37]

In concluding his remarks, Justice Field wrote:

> If the provisions of the Constitution can be set aside by an act of Congress, where is the course of usurpation to end? The present assault upon capital is but the beginning. It will be but the stepping-stone to others, larger and more sweeping, till our political contests will become a war of the poor against the rich; a war constantly growing in intensity and bitterness.[38]

C. Corporate Tax Ruled an Excise Tax

Although the income tax act of 1894 was deemed unconstitutional, Justice Field's prediction, i.e., "[the] present assault upon capital is but the beginning," came true with the passage of the Corporation Tax Law on August 5, 1909. As with the 1894 income tax act, the constitutionality of this law was also challenged and was ultimately decided by the Supreme Court on March 13, 1911.

In *Flint*, the Supreme Court ruled that a tax on corporations was "an excise tax on the privilege of doing business in a corporate capacity," which was measured by income. Therefore, since an

---

37 *Id*. at 589 & 826.
38 *Id*. at 607.

excise tax was an indirect tax, the apportionment limitation did not apply. Accordingly, the tax was deemed constitutional.[39]

Professor Tribe insists that the Supreme Court reversed itself for the second time in *Flint* but, the "confusion was put to an end in 1913 with the ratification of the Sixteenth Amendment..."[40]

---

39 Flint v. Stone Tracy Co., 220 U.S. 107 (1911).
40 Tribe, supra note 25.

IV. ESTABLISHING A NEW PARADIGM

What Professor Tribe is referring to with respect to his statement that the Supreme Court reversed itself for the second time is that in 1880, in *Springer*,[41] the Supreme Court ruled that a tax on the income of an individual was not a direct tax; then in 1895, in *Pollock* (discussed supra), they ruled that a tax on incomes was a direct tax as long as the source of the income was property; then in *Flint* (discussed supra), they reversed themselves for a second time; and, stated that a tax on corporations, measured by income, was an indirect tax for the privilege of doing business in corporate form.[42]

By stating his case as he did, i.e. the Supreme Court reversed itself a second time, it made it easier for him to conclude that all was well-settled when the 16th Amendment was ratified.

It might be more appropriate to say that the Supreme Court erred in *Springer*, got it right or corrected their mistake in *Pollock*; and, properly concluded in *Flint* that a tax on corporations, measured by income, is an excise or indirect tax for the privilege of doing business in corporate form. Furthermore, the 16th Amendment has not eliminated confusion as so stated by Professor Tribe, it has caused confusion; and, has contributed to the steady erosion

---

41 See Springer v. U.S. 102 U.S. 586 (1880).
42 Tribe, supra note 25.

of our rights as set forth in the Constitution, in particular, the Bill of Rights.

Before proceeding with a discussion of the tax issues involved, it may be pertinent for the reader to understand just how Professor Tribe feels about our Founders and Constitution; and, where he may be coming from, so to speak, when he failed to adequately address these issues in his treatise on "American Constitutional Law."

According to Professor Tribe, "... to defy popular will in order to do what they [i.e. unelected judges and elected officials] believe the Constitution requires... raise questions of legitimacy... [T]hose who were framers and ratifiers most assuredly could not be said to speak for any current majority, much less for today's people as a whole.[43] On the contrary, it is vital that we not lose sight of just how imperfect, and often highly objectionable, our Constitution remains."[44]

In addition, he refers to our Founders as a "highly limited constituency of white property owners... with whom most of us have only the most limited link (if any at all), [who decided] to limit our future freedom to exercise power..."[45]

Therefore, Professor Tribe suggests, "... sometimes meanings are subject to chronic flux. In particular, documents of considerable... importance—like the Constitution—may themselves give new importance to terms previously the beneficiaries of easy consensus, and thereby open the meaning of such terms to new debate."[46]

---

43 Tribe, supra note 25, at 18.

44 Tribe, supra note 25, at 21.

45 Tribe, supra note 25, at 20-24.

46 Tribe, supra note 25, at 62.

And finally, Professor Tribe explains:

> The upshot is that the Constitution's text, and historical material relevant to the text's proper understanding, will almost invariably recede into the background behind a parade of precedents, until the Constitution itself begins to seem 'rather like... a remote ancestor who came over on the Mayflower.' As Robert Post has rightly observed, beginners in constitutional law are often amazed by how little of the Constitution they find in constitutional opinions, which tend to be filled with the elaboration and application of various doctrinal 'tests' extracted from prior decisions.[47]

I find it interesting that we continue to study the works or writings of Aristotle, Plato, Homer's The Iliad and The Odyssey, and other similar works that were written centuries before our founding; and, our Scholars seem to be able to preserve the original understanding and meanings of what was being conveyed. Yet, certain Constitutional Scholars and members of the legal profession find it extremely difficult to find and understand the original meaning and intent of our founding documents that are, at most, 231-to-250 years old. Furthermore, as suggested by Professor Tribe, these meanings appear to be in a state of continual change. If this is the case, it appears we may have progressed from "the rule of kings or man" to the "rule of law" in 1776; and, back to the "rule of kings or man" today.

According to Dr. Williams, "During earlier periods, Congress and the Supreme Court had far greater respect for the Constitution. They understood that if the federal government was to have a power not delegated, or expressly forbidden, by the Constitution they had to use the provisions of Article V to gain that power

---

47 Tribe, supra note 25, at 84.

by amendment." For example, in 1919 Congress understood that to prohibit the sale of alcohol, it required the passage of the Eighteenth Amendment. "Today, it's an entirely different story. Congress, the White House and the Supreme Court have abiding contempt for the Constitution and we Americans are left with a constitutional carcass."[48]

As Dr. Williams points out, "No matter what you think about the alcohol prohibitionists, we can have a bit of admiration for them because they used the constitutional route to get their agenda across."[49] Whereas, today, "constitutional stealth" (e.g., taxation, majority votes for legislation and "totalitarian tactics" of agencies like the EPA, FDA and IRS) seems to be employed to circumvent the Constitution; and, thereby, avoiding the amendment process required by Article V.[50]

Dr. Williams continues, "…the education establishment has played a greater role through the dumbing down of Americans. The resulting ignorance has allowed us to let charlatans and quacks in the legal profession tell us what the Constitution means."[51]

Unlike Professor Tribe, who seems to believe that the Constitution is "considerably" complex,[52] Dr. Williams rightly states that, "[t]he Constitution was not written for intellectual elites; it was

---

48 Walter E. Williams, Professor of Economics at George Mason University, *Constitutional Corruption*, Oct. 4, 1995, http://www.gmu.edu/departments/ economics/wew/articles/95/Constitutional-Corruption.htm.

49 *Id.*

50 *Id.* Dr. Williams did not specifically refer to taxation or the IRS in this particular article. However, he has done so in numerous other articles dealing more specifically with taxation. His articles can be accessed through the following website: http://www.gmu.edu/departments/economics/wew/ articles.html.

51 Williams, supra note 48.

52 Tribe, supra note 25, at 62.

understandable to a nation of mostly farmers at the time it was written."[53]

And, Professor Epstein states,

> The point here is that anyone on any side of the political spectrum can play fast and loose with authoritative text, and those evasions are no more palatable when done by one side or the other. The Progressives were wrong on matters of constitutional interpretation because they consciously used their intellectual powers to rewrite, not understand, key provisions of the constitutional text.[54]

Furthermore, Professor Barnett appears to agree with Professors Williams and Epstein:

> Since the adoption of the Constitution, courts have eliminated clause after clause that interfered with the exercise of government power... As a result of judicial decisions, [certain] provisions of the Constitution are now largely gone and, in their absence, the enacted Constitution has been lost and even forgotten... The Constitution that was actually enacted and formally amended creates islands

---

53 Williams, supra note 48.

54 Richard A. Epstein, How Progressives Rewrote the Constitution, 136 (2006). In his introduction, Professor Epstein states, "The Progressives were the self-conscious social and legal reformers who occupied center stage in the period roughly from the onset of the 20th century through the election of Franklin Delano Roosevelt as president in 1932. They exerted a considerable influence on legal and constitutional theory in the years before Roosevelt took over the presidency... Progressives believed in the power of science and economics, employed by government, to lift up the economic and social position of the general population... they were influenced... by Bismarckian social initiatives in 19th-century Germany, which had pioneered various forms of worker protection and social insurance." In his Preface, Professor Epstein says, "There is no easy metric... of what... should be done to correct past constitutional errors".

of government powers in a sea of liberty. The judicially redacted constitution creates islands of liberty rights in a sea of governmental powers. Judicial redaction has created a substantially different constitution from the one written on parchment that resides under glass in Washington. Though that Constitution is now lost, it has not been repealed, so it could be found again.[55]

Professor Barnett continues, "All this has been done knowingly by judges and their academic enablers who think they can improve upon the original Constitution and substitute for it one that is superior."[56]

According to Professor Barnett, "... many constitutional scholars write as though we are not bound by the actual words of the Constitution because those words are obstacles to noble objectives... by subtly undercutting the legitimacy of the Constitution while at the same time preserving its much-revered form, a judge or even a clever constitutional scholar can become the man behind the curtain... This is a fraud on the public."[57]

And finally, as so aptly put by Professor Barnett, "The Constitution is a law designed to restrict the lawmakers."[58] Whereas today, it has been used, when convenient, and ignored when appropriate, to trample individual rights for the good of society as a whole. And, who determines what is good for society... those who have the political power and clout.

---

55 Randy E. Barnett, Restoring the Lost Constitution; The Presumption of Liberty, 1 (2004).

56 *Id.* at 1-2.

57 Barnett, supra note 55, at 2.

58 Barnett, supra note 55, at 103.

Therefore, we all should keep in mind the words of Thomas Jefferson, "Whenever a man has cast a longing eye on offices, a rottenness begins in his conduct."[59]

The point being, if we did not have lawyers, judges, and legal scholars, with views similar to Professor Tribe's, whose real intentions appear to be to circumvent the limitations set forth in the U.S. Constitution, when it suits their political agenda, chances are this thesis would not be necessary.

Consequently, when an individual has been brought up and educated within a certain system, such a person becomes use to a given paradigm, i.e. "the prevailing view of things." Accordingly, the purpose of the foregoing discussion is to assist the reader in either establishing a new paradigm and/or keeping an open-mind when reviewing the remainder of this thesis.

---

59 Thomas Jefferson, Quotations of Thomas Jefferson (1743-1826), compiled by Applewood Books, Inc., 29 (2003).

V. THE INCOME TAX FROM 1895 THROUGH RATIFICATION OF THE SIXTEENTH AMENDMENT

A. Summary of the Pollock Decision

In *Pollock* (discussed supra), the Supreme Court ruled that a tax on incomes was a direct tax as long as the source of the income was property; and, therefore, since the tax was not apportioned, it was unconstitutional and void. According to Professor Jensen:

> The Income Tax Cases proved to be extremely contentious; it took two sets of hearings and opinions for the Court to strike down the entire taxing statute, and the Court was divided each time. In the first case (*Pollock I*[60]), the Court, by a 6-2 vote, invalidated the tax only insofar as it was imposed on income from real property. The Court accepted the *Hylton*[61] dictum that a tax on real estate is a direct tax and saw no constitutionally significant difference between a tax on real estate and a tax on income from real estate.[62]

---

60 Pollock v. Farmers' Loan & Trust Co., 157 U.S. 429 (1895).

61 Hylton v. U.S., 3 U.S. 171 (1796).

62 Erik. M. Jensen, Professor of Law at Case Western Reserve University, *The Taxing Power, the Sixteenth Amendment, and the Meaning of "Incomes"*, 1071, 33 Ariz. St. L.J. 1057 (Winter 2001).

Professor Jensen continues:

> Proponents of the tax didn't like it, but Chief Justice Fuller actually did a nice job of tying his analysis to *Hylton*: to the extent this was a tax on real property, it had to be apportioned. Fuller provided other justifications as well for rejecting the tax on income from real property. He looked to how shiftable the tax was, a point with support in eighteenth century understanding...[63]

According to Chief Justice Fuller:

> Ordinarily all taxes paid primarily by persons who can shift the burden upon some one else, or who are under no legal compulsion to pay them, are considered indirect taxes; but a tax upon property holders in respect of their estates, whether real or personal, or of the income yielded by such estates, and the payment of which cannot be avoided, are direct taxes.[64]

Professor Jensen further explains:

> And the apportionment rule, wrote Fuller, was a response to the deficiency of the requisitions process: "There were no means of compulsion, as Congress had no power whatever to lay any tax upon individuals." With the power to tax individuals came a check on that power—apportionment. As Fuller emphasized, "The men who framed and adopted [the Constitution] had just emerged from the struggle for independence whose rallying cry had been that 'taxation and representation go together.'"

---

63 *Id.* at 1072.

64 See supra note 60, at 558.

Because it dealt only with income from real property, *Pollock I* left the status of a large part of the 1894 income tax in limbo, and the Court was pressured to rehear the case. In *Pollock II*,[65] heard several months later, the Court held (barely, 5-4) that income from personal property should be treated the same as income from real property. It would make no sense to require apportionment of a tax on rents, but not a tax on dividends and interest.

With income from property removed from the base of an unapportioned tax, and because of the high exemption amount effectively exempted the ordinary services-provider from the scope of the law, the tax was gutted. The five-justice majority therefore concluded the entire statute had to fall, including the part on earned income…[66]

B. Capitation Taxes Include a Tax on the Wages of Labor

Therefore, as a result of the decision in *Pollock*, the entire income tax act of 1894 was ruled unconstitutional because a tax on property, and a tax on the income of the property, was determined to be a direct tax, which had not been apportioned.

Although Chief Justice Fuller did an excellent job of defining what direct and indirect taxes were, the 5-4 majority opinion left the definition of direct taxes open to question, with the exception of taxes on property and the income from that property.

However, buried within *Pollock I*, Mr. George F. Edmunds' brief contains some information and a definition of capitation taxes,

---

65 Pollock v. Farmers' Loan & Trust Co., 158 U.S. 601 (1895).

66 Jensen, supra note 62, at 1072.

which is extremely important; and, was not addressed in *Pollock* or any other Supreme Court case that I am currently aware of.

According to Article I, Section 9, "No Capitation, or other direct, Tax shall be laid, unless in Proportion to the Census or Enumeration herein before directed to be taken."[67] Therefore, if a certain tax is deemed to represent a Capitation Tax, it must be apportioned for it to be constitutional. And, as stated supra, the apportionment requirement makes such a tax impractical.

In his brief, Mr. Edmund stated:

> It is curious that in old English times, and in the law dictionaries, even since the Constitution was formed, an income tax was described as a capitation tax imposed upon persons in consideration of the amount of their property and their profits... that a tax upon the person in respect of his income did not fall within the category of the words, duties, imposts, and excises, but that it fell within the terms and description of capitation and other direct taxes...

> Every dictionary shows—I have looked at Johnson's dictionary—the great dictionary at that time—and in Jacob's, of the editions of those dates, and in the Acts of Parliament, and in Blackstone, and in Coke, and everywhere this distinction [i.e. taxes assessed against the income of an individual is a Capitation Tax] appears in the clearest way.[68]

Furthermore, Chief Justice Fuller stated that, in rendering their opinion, they must enquire as to what were recognized as direct taxes at the time the Constitution was "framed and adopted."

67 See supra note 18.
68 See supra note 60.

And, in so doing, he stated that Adam Smith's "Wealth of Nations" was published in 1776, inferring that it was a source in determining what were considered direct taxes at that time.[69]

In addition, Drs. Munro and Klieforth have stated that the Scottish Enlightenment (1730-1790) had a significant influence on our Founders; and, the economist Adam Smith, was one of the "great philosophers" of that period.[70] Furthermore,

> James Madison and James Wilson, the second of the two native-born Scots to sign the Declaration, were principal co-authors of the Federal Constitution of 1787. Both men were schooled in the Scottish Enlightenment... Indeed, Witherspoon, the teacher of Madison, had studied with... Adam Smith... The schooling of Madison, Hamilton and Jefferson was remarkably similar in terms of education and instruction by Scots.[71]

Also, when Madison was asked what his favorite books for a congressional library would be, Adam Smith's, "The Wealth of Nations," made the list.[72]

According to Adam Smith, taxes on the "wages of labour" are direct taxes; and, "[a]bsurd and destructive as such taxes are, however, they take place in many countries."[73] With respect to Capitation Taxes, Adam Smith said:

---

69 See supra note 60, at 559.

70 Alexander Leslie Klieforth and Robert John Munro, The Scottish Invention of America, Democracy and Human Rights, 213 (2004).

71 *Id.* at 269.

72 *Id.* at 270.

73 Adam Smith, The Wealth of Nations (1776), 994, Regnery Publishing, Inc. (1998).

Capitation taxes, if it is attempted to proportion them to the fortune or revenue of each contributor, become altogether arbitrary. The state of a man's fortune varies from day to day, and without an inquisition more intolerable than any tax, and renewed at least once every year, can only be guessed at...[74]

Capitation taxes... are direct taxes upon the wages of labour, and are attended with all the inconveniences of such taxes.[75]

Therefore, a tax assessed against the salary and wages or self-employment income of an individual is a direct capitation tax which can only be constitutional if it is apportioned. For, as Thomas Jefferson stated, the government they established did not contemplate a tax on the wages of labor, i.e. "... a wise and frugal government... shall not take from the mouth of labor the bread it has earned."[76]

C. Status of the Income Tax Prior to the Sixteenth Amendment

To summarize, with the decision in *Pollock*, the 1894 income tax was ruled unconstitutional and void. However, the decision left open the question of what other taxes may be considered direct taxes; and, thereby, subject to apportionment in order to be constitutional.

The reason Chief Justice Fuller did not continue his analysis with respect to earned income is most likely because the exemption was very high at the time, i.e. $4,000; and, the tax rate was only

74 *Id.* at 996.

75 *Id.* at 999.

76 Jefferson, supra note 14.

two percent, thereby affecting very few taxpayers in just a few states.[77] In addition, the remaining justices were "equally divided, and, therefore, no opinion [was] expressed"[78] since the entire statute could be struck-down, because the income from property was an un-apportioned direct tax.

Therefore, in 1895 and up through March 13, 1911, an income tax did not exist. However, in *Flint* (discussed supra), the Supreme Court ruled that a corporate income tax was an excise tax, measured by income, for the privilege of operating a business in corporate form.

Accordingly, prior to the adoption of the 16th Amendment, a tax on the incomes of an individual and on any property, real or personal, should have been considered a direct tax subject to the apportionment requirement. The only exception was an income tax on corporations, which was deemed an excise or indirect tax for "the privilege of doing business in a corporate capacity."[79]

---

77 Jensen, supra note 62, at 1070.
78 See supra note 60, at 586.
79 See supra note 39.

VI. THE SIXTEENTH AMENDMENT

A. What It Says and Its' Purpose

The 16th Amendment states, "The Congress shall have the power to lay and collect taxes on incomes, from whatever source derived, without apportionment among the several States, and without regard to any census or enumeration."[80] In my opinion, it is not so much what it says, it is more important as to what it does not say or do, i.e., it does not state that it supersedes or is superior to any other provisions in the Constitution. And, in fact, Supreme Court Justice White made a similar statement in 1916.

In fact, there were three cases decided concerning the 16th Amendment, all by Chief Justice White. The first, *Brushaber*,[81] was decided on January 24, 1916; and, the other two, *Stanton*[82] and *Tyee Realty*,[83] following the reasoning in *Brushaber*, were both decided on February 21, 1916. In *Brushaber*, Justice White stated:

> We are of the opinion, however, that the confusion is not inherent, but rather arises from the conclusion that the Sixteenth Amendment provides for a hitherto unknown power of taxation, that is, a power to levy an income tax which although direct should not be subject to the

---

80 U.S. Const. amend. XVI.
81 Brushaber v. Union Pacific Railroad Co., 240 U.S. 1 (1916).
82 Stanton v. Baltic Mining Co., 240 U.S. 103 (1916).
83 Tyee Realty Co. v. Anderson, 240 U.S. 115 (1916).

regulation of apportionment applicable to all other direct taxes. And the far-reaching effect of this erroneous assumption will be made clear…[84]

What Justice White just said was that the 16th Amendment did not authorize Congress to "levy an income tax which [is a direct tax to begin with; and, not make it] subject to the regulation of apportionment applicable to all other direct taxes."

In other words, if an income tax is a direct tax to begin with, the 16th Amendment does not authorize Congress to dispense with the apportionment requirement.

Said another way, if you cannot tax real estate directly without being subject to the apportionment requirement, the 16th Amendment allows Congress to tax the income from the real estate, without the apportionment requirement, because the income from the real estate was indirect from the beginning.

Justice White continues and explains why this is so:

> …the proposition and the contentions [i.e. that the Amendment allows Congress to tax income, that is Direct from the beginning, without apportionment] …if acceded to, would cause one provision of the Constitution to destroy another; that is they would result in bringing the provisions of the Amendment exempting a direct tax from apportionment into irreconcilable conflict with the general requirement that all direct taxes be apportioned. This result…would create radical and destructive changes in our constitutional system and multiply confusion.[85]

---

84 See supra note 81, at 11.

85 See supra note 81, at 12.

And finally, he says that the purpose of the 16th Amendment was to overturn the decision in *Pollock*; and, not to create a new tax on income, as a direct tax relieved from apportionment, "thus destroying the two great classifications [direct taxes subject to apportionment and indirect taxes] which have been recognized and enforced from the beginning…"[86]

In other words, and as explained by Justice White, the 16th Amendment does not say that it supersedes or is superior to or, for that matter, amends Article I, Section 9 which states, "No Capitation, or other direct, Tax shall be laid, unless in Proportion to the Census or Enumeration herein before directed to be taken."

Accordingly, if an income tax would be deemed a direct tax (e.g., capitation tax and/or a tax on the wages of labor), from the beginning, it must be apportioned in accordance with Article I, Section 9. However, if an income tax is indirect, from the beginning, e.g., income (indirect) from real estate (direct), then the income tax levied against the income from the real estate is not subject to the apportionment requirement as set forth in the 16th Amendment.

Again, as Justice White explained, Congress was granted no new taxing powers by the 16th Amendment; and, its purpose was to overturn the decision in *Pollock*, which was to prevent an otherwise indirect tax from being considered a direct tax based on the source of the income.

Therefore, if an income tax would be deemed a direct tax, from the beginning, apportionment is required under Article I, Section 9 because the 16th Amendment does not supersede it, nor is it superior to this section of the Constitution. The only thing

---

86 See supra note 81, at 18-19 & 242.

that the 16th Amendment did is relieve the obligation to look to the source of the income; and, if the source was direct, then the income from that source would also be direct as decided in *Pollock*.

B. The Prevailing View

As, I hope, has been made clear, the 16th Amendment did not give Congress any new and unrestricted taxing powers. It only granted them the ability to tax, without apportionment, income that was already considered indirect, without having to consider the source of the income, which may be direct; and, thereby, making apportionment necessary under *Pollock*. Again, the 16th Amendment only over-ruled *Pollock*... it did not replace the requirements set forth in Article I, Sections 8 and 9, with respect to apportionment of direct taxes and uniformity for indirect taxes. Furthermore, and to be explained later, it does not supersede, nor is it superior to any other provisions set forth in the Constitution.

However, the "conventional wisdom" ignores the problems and limitations discussed supra. In addition, it is best illustrated, by looking at Professor Tribe's coverage of "The Taxing Power," relating to these specific issues, in his treatise on constitutional law. He devotes less than three pages to the subject; does not acknowledge the decision in *Brushaber*; and states, "The confusion was put to an end in 1913 with the ratification of the Sixteenth Amendment..."[87]

Professor Jensen's view of the situation appears to differ from Professor Tribe:

---

87 Tribe, supra note 25, at 841-843.

The conventional wisdom might be a generally correct description of things-as-they-are, but it reflects a peculiar theory of constitutional interpretation. It doesn't comport with the original understanding of the Sixteenth Amendment... and it doesn't comport with any modern theory that takes restrictions on governmental power seriously.[88]

In other words, the "conventional wisdom" is wrong. And, as suggested by Professor Barnett, such actions, e.g., failing to adequately address the relevant issues, undercut the legitimacy of the Constitution, thereby perpetrating "a fraud on the public."[89]

Furthermore, it is interesting to note that Professor Tribe devotes approximately twenty-two pages to former President Bill Clinton's impeachment,[90] while less than 3 pages concerning the taxing power and the 16th Amendment.[91]

Even though, Congress, through its' taxing powers, has an impact on every American every day of our lives, while a presidential impeachment, although newsworthy and entertaining, does not affect the average person. This appears to be a good example of what Professor Barnett describes as a constitutional scholar subtly undercutting the legitimacy of the Constitution through distraction and subterfuge.[92]

In over 38 years of teaching at Harvard[93], how many students, lawyers, and judges have been taught, by Professor Tribe, that the

---

88 See Jensen, supra note 62, at 1061.
89 See Barnett, supra note 55, at 2.
90 Tribe, supra note 25, at 181-202.
91 Tribe, supra note 25, at 841-843.
92 See Barnett, supra note 55, at 2.
93 http://en.wikipedia.org/wiki/Laurence_Tribe.

16th Amendment gave Congress the power to define incomes and tax indiscriminately without any real restrictions imposed upon them? In addition, Professor Tribe first came out with his treatise on "American Constitutional Law" in 1978.[94] How many other Universities and Law Schools used his text; and, whose students also received the same biased instruction?

C. Confusion within the Courts and the IRS

Professor Tribe's statement that the confusion was ended with the ratification of the 16th Amendment may be what he desires, but, it is not very accurate. According to Mr. Becraft:

> Confusion abounds as to the correct interpretation of *Brushaber*, and this is obvious because various courts of this nation have relied upon this line of authority to reach diametrically opposing results.
>
> The state courts have been particularly split over the nature of an income tax and whether it constitutes a direct property tax or an indirect/excise, which is not imposed on property. A small number of them hold that an income tax is a direct property tax... A far larger number of state courts disagree... and have held that an income tax is not a property tax but an excise...
>
> This split of authority evident within the state cases also manifests itself in the federal appellate courts... in the First Circuit it is difficult to determine the meaning of the 16th Amendment because... that court held that the "16th Amendment eliminated the indirect/direct distinction as applied to taxes on income." Next door in the Second Circuit, there is uncertainty revealed by three completely

---

94 *Id.*

inconsistent cases... In the Third Circuit, it has been held in one case that all income taxes are direct, but in another that only some are direct...

In the remainder of the Circuits, the difference of opinion as to whether the federal income tax is a direct or indirect tax is likewise as profound and confusing. In the Fourth and Sixth Circuits, the income tax has been held to be an excise tax... However, in the Fifth, Seventh, Eighth and Tenth Circuits, arguments that this tax is an excise have been squarely rejected and determined to be frivolous...

Therefore, while the Supreme Court rejected in *Baltic* the argument that "the 16ᵗʰ Amendment authorized only an exceptional direct income tax without apportionment," this position now prevails in the Fifth, Seventh, Eighth and Tenth Circuits. In the Second Circuit, the existing authority illogically claims that the tax is both.[95]

In his brief, Mr. Becraft cites his authorities for the statements he made, which have not been verified, with the exception of one case that will be discussed below; and, my reading of the *Baltic* decision agrees with his. Furthermore, in 1989, Mr. Becraft was fined $2,500 for filing a "frivolous petition for rehearing" with the Ninth Circuit Court of Appeals.[96] According to the Court, Mr. Becraft's frivolous argument could be reduced to "one elemental proposition: The Sixteenth Amendment does not authorize a direct non-apportioned income tax on resident United States citizens... We hardly need comment on the patent absurdity and frivolity of such a position."

---

95 Becraft, supra note 2.
96 In Re Becraft, 885 F.2d 547 (9ᵗʰ Cir. 1989).

The Court continues, "For over 75 years, the Supreme Court and lower federal courts have both implicitly and explicitly recognized the Sixteenth Amendment's authorization of a non-apportioned direct income tax…" After making such a statement, i.e. the 16th Amendment authorizes a non-apportioned direct income tax, the Court then cites *Brushaber*[97] without apparently reading Justice White's opinion.

In *Brushaber*, Justice White specifically said that such a statement, or rather, assumption, was erroneous.[98] In other words, the Ninth Circuit Court of Appeals had no idea what it was talking about regarding this issue. Furthermore, because they have been getting it wrong for 75 years, an incorrect interpretation apparently becomes the standard used by the Court, not only in the Ninth Circuit, but, in practically all the circuits as demonstrated by Mr. Becraft supra.

Furthermore, the IRS latched onto this same erroneous statement, in their discussion of frivolous arguments: "Contention: The Sixteenth Amendment does not authorize a direct non-apportioned federal income tax on United States citizens." According to the IRS, this contention is incorrect and frivolous.[99] Following is the IRS position statement on this issue:

> Some assert that the Sixteenth Amendment does not authorize a direct non-apportioned income tax and thus, U.S. citizens and residents are not subject to federal income tax laws.
>
> The Law: The courts have both implicitly and explicitly recognized that the Sixteenth Amendment authorizes

---

97 *Id.* at 4 - 5.

98 See supra note 81, at 11-12.

99 The Truth About Frivolous Arguments, 30 (11/30/2006), http://www.irs.gov/pub/irs-utl/friv_tax.pdf.

a non-apportioned direct income tax on United States citizens and that the federal tax laws as applied are valid. In *United States v. Collins*, 920 F2d 619, 629 (10th Cir. 1990), *cert. denied*, 500 U.S. 920 (1991), the court cited to *Brushaber v. Union Pac. R.R.*, 240 U.S. 1, 12-19 (1916), and noted that the U.S. Supreme Court has recognized that the "sixteenth amendment authorizes a direct nonapportioned tax upon United States citizens throughout the nation."[100]

Unfortunately, with respect to the case[101] cited by the IRS, as is typical, the Defendant, and in this particular situation, his Attorney, who was granted *pro hac vice* status, which was later revoked,[102] were "off-the-wall tax protestors."[103] As with most of these cases, the defendants throw every conceivable argument at the court; and, most are indeed frivolous. Accordingly, as in this particular situation, a legitimate argument gets lumped in with all the other frivolous and outrageous statements, i.e. the Attorney for the Defendant, among the frivolous positions, argued that the 16th Amendment did not authorize a direct non-apportioned tax on U.S. citizens.[104] This statement is absolutely correct when your authority is *Brushaber*, as the Court said it was.[105]

However, the Court contradicted the ruling in *Brushaber* as follows: "For seventy-five years, the Supreme Court has recognized that the sixteenth amendment authorizes a direct nonapportioned tax upon United States citizens... see *Brushaber*...

---

100 *Id.*
101 United States v. Collins, 920 F. 2d 619 (10th Cir. 1990).
102 *Id.*
103 Jensen, supra note 62, at 1064.
104 See supra note 101, at 29.
105 *Id.*

efforts to argue otherwise have been sanctioned as frivolous...[106] Did they read *Brushaber*... apparently not.

Here's what Justice White actually said about a direct non-apportioned income tax:

> We are of the opinion, however, that the confusion is not inherent, but rather arises from the conclusion that the Sixteenth Amendment provides for a hitherto unknown power of taxation, that is, a power to levy an income tax which although direct should not be subject to the regulation of apportionment applicable to all other direct taxes. And the far-reaching effect of this erroneous assumption will be made clear...[107]

> ...the proposition and the contentions [i.e. that the Amendment allows Congress to tax income, that is Direct from the beginning, without apportionment] ...if acceded to, would cause one provision of the Constitution to destroy another; that is they would result in bringing the provisions of the Amendment exempting a direct tax from apportionment into irreconcilable conflict with the general requirement that all direct taxes be apportioned. This result...would create radical and destructive changes in our constitutional system and multiply confusion.[108]

> [Furthermore]... the Amendment was drawn for the purpose of doing away... with the principle upon which the Pollock Case was decided, that is, whether a tax on income was direct not by a consideration of... the taxed

---

106 *Id.*

107 See supra note 81, at 11.

108 See supra note 81, at 12.

income... but... on the property from which the income was derived...[109]

Therefore, according to *Brushaber*, both the IRS and the 10th Circuit Court of Appeals are wrong when they state that the 16th Amendment authorizes a direct non-apportioned tax. The reason was explained by Justice White. If the 16th Amendment allowed a direct non-apportioned income tax, it would be in conflict with Article I, Section 9 requiring all direct taxes to be subject to the apportionment rule. Furthermore, if the intent of the 16th Amendment was to amend or change the requirements set forth in Article I, Section 9, it would have to say so.

And, as explained by Justice White, the purpose of the 16th Amendment was to avoid the *Pollock* principle; and, allow Congress to tax incomes, which are considered indirect from the beginning, without having to look to the source of the income, which may be direct, thereby converting the indirect income tax to a direct income tax subject to the rule of apportionment.

The issue is not whether or not the 16th Amendment allows a non-apportioned direct income tax—it did not according to the ruling in *Brushaber*—the issue should be whether or not the income tax is a direct or indirect tax. As discussed supra, in *Flint*, the Supreme Court ruled that the income tax represented an indirect excise tax for the privilege of doing business in corporate form. Furthermore, as was decided in *Pollock*, a tax on real estate was a direct tax; and, the income from the real estate was also deemed a direct tax. However, the 16th Amendment overturned the *Pollock* principle; and, although a tax on real estate would be a direct tax, a tax on the income from real estate is now an indirect tax.

---

109 See supra note 81, at 242.

But, when the government desires to tax individuals directly, the situation is, or rather, should be quite different based on the original understanding of the Constitution.

According to Justice Fuller:

> Nothing can be clearer than what the Constitution intended to guard against was the exercise by the general government of the power of directly taxing persons and property within any State through a majority made up from the other States...and was manifestly designed to operate to restrain the exercise of the power of direct taxation to extraordinary emergencies, and to prevent an attack upon accumulated property by mere force of numbers.[110]

Further, in a publication from1796, Albert Gallatin wrote: "The most generally received opinion, however, is that by direct taxes in the Constitution, those are meant which are raised on the capital or revenue of the people; by indirect, such as are raised on their expense."[111] In addition, taxes assessed against the income of an individual were considered a capitation tax.[112] And, more specifically, a tax assessed against the wages of labor was a capitation tax.[113] Furthermore, wages for labor is the "classic form of property."[114] In other words, taxing the income of an individual is a direct tax subject to apportionment based on the original understanding of the Constitution; and, should be so today, in spite of the 16th Amendment.

---

110 See supra note 29, at 820.
111 See supra note 29, at 570.
112 See supra note 60, George F. Edmund's brief.
113 Smith, supra note 73, at 999.
114 Finn, supra note 119.

The purpose of the above discussion, however, is to let the reader know that, in spite of what Professor Tribe and others have tried to convey, including the Judiciary and the IRS, the 16th Amendment did not eliminate confusion, it significantly increased it.

In addition, it may be appropriate to see what Judge Winter had to say regarding the income tax in a criminal case that was appealed in the Fourth Circuit:

> We hold that defendant must be exonerated from the charges lodged against her. As a matter of law, defendant cannot be guilty of willfully evading and defeating income taxes on income, the taxability of which is so uncertain that even coordinate branches of the United States Government plausibly reach directly opposing conclusions. As a matter of law, the requisite intent to evade and defeat income taxes is missing. The obligation to pay is so problematical that defendant's actual intent is irrelevant. Even if she had consulted the law and sought to guide herself accordingly, she could have no certainty as to what the law required.
>
> It is settled that when the law is vague or highly debatable, a defendant, actually or imputedly, lacks the requisite intent to violate it...[115]

And finally, much to the chagrin of certain constitutional scholars, the 16th Amendment, as demonstrated above, has created much confusion. For, as Senator Elihu Root stated during the debate on the first income tax act passed following the ratification of the 16th Amendment:

> I guess you will have to go to jail. If that is the result of not understanding the Income Tax Law I shall meet you

---

115 United States v. Critzer, 498 F.2d 1160, 7, (4th Cir. 1974).

there. We shall have a merry, merry time, for all of our friends will be there. It will be an intellectual center, for no one understands the Income Tax Law except persons who have not sufficient intelligence to understand the questions that arise under it.[116]

D. The Meaning of "Incomes"

Getting back to the 16th Amendment, we find that Congress has the "power to lay and collect taxes on incomes."[117] It does not say that Congress can define the term "incomes" and change the definition whenever it is desirable. Yet, that is exactly what has been happening.

The term "incomes" had a specific meaning when the 16th Amendment was proposed and ratified; and, that is the meaning that it should have today. If Congress wants to change that meaning; and, redefine it at whim, it must do so in accordance with the amendment process outlined in Article V of the Constitution.[118]

For many years now, Professor Jensen has been rightly arguing "that the history leading to the Sixteenth Amendment gives content to the meaning of "taxes on incomes."[119] In his article written in 2001, he responds "to claims the sky will fall if, all of a sudden, we take into account constitutional issues that have been ignored for decades."[120]

---

116 Becraft, supra note 2.
117 See supra note 80.
118 Williams, supra note 48 and U.S. Const. art. V.
119 Jensen, supra note 62, at 1058.
120 Jensen, supra note 62, at 1064.

If this last statement is true, and I believe it is, the actions taken by Congress and the complicity of our Judiciary should be appalling to anyone who has any respect for our Constitution, our Founders, and the "rule of law."

As stated by Professor Jensen:

> Nothing in the constitutional text, or in constitutional debates, suggests the Constitution's primary limits on the national taxing power, the uniformity rule and the direct-tax apportionment rule, were intended to be window-dressing.

> No matter how much an individual Federalist like Alexander Hamilton favored an unlimited taxing power, no one argued in public for that position, and with good reason. Such an argument would have been fatal to the Constitution.

> The American population wouldn't have accepted a Constitution understood to permit all sorts of taxation without limitation, not after the Revolutionary War. In the late eighteenth century, Americans had every reason to fear an unlimited taxing power.[121]

Furthermore, Professor Jensen agrees that the term "direct taxes" … "was originally understood to encompass a substantial universe of potential levies."[122] And, "direct taxation was feared by most founders."[123]

---

121 Jensen, supra note 62, at 1069.
122 *Id.*
123 Jensen, supra note 62, at 1068.

E. Limitations and Opinion

To summarize, the Supreme Court held, in *Brushaber*, that the purpose of the 16th Amendment was not to authorize an un-apportioned direct tax, but rather, to prevent the application of the *Pollock* principle, so that an otherwise valid indirect tax would not be construed as being a direct tax.

Furthermore, Congress was not granted any additional taxing powers under the 16th Amendment… only that a valid indirect or excise tax would not be construed as being a direct tax by looking at the source of the income.

In addition, the term "taxes on incomes" has a meaning; and, Congress has no business redefining this constitutional term whenever they so desire. The meaning is the one that existed when the 16th Amendment was proposed and ratified; and, it related to profits, e.g., no income existed if the financial activity resulted in a loss. However, this concept, the meaning of "incomes," does not have to be defined for purposes of this thesis. It is only important to point out that "incomes" is a constitutional term; and, Congress and the IRS have continually been exceeding their authority by redefining this term.

Also, taxes that are levied against corporate activity are easily justified because a corporation is a creation of the legislature; and, as such, any activity that it engages in can be excised, even if the same activity, when engaged in by an individual can not.

But, we have a very different situation when it comes to levying taxes upon the individual. As alluded to in *Pollock*, and based on historical information, income taxes assessed against an individual was considered a direct tax from the beginning; and, therefore, would not be subject to the 16th Amendment, and, any such tax must be apportioned to be constitutional.

In addition, wages for labor was and is property;[124] and, the taxing of such wages was considered a capitation tax subject to the rule of apportionment. This issue, I do believe, has never been properly litigated, i.e. wages for labor represents a capitation tax subject to apportionment.

Accordingly, it is my opinion that an individual, at a minimum, whose sole income is derived from salary and wages, or from self-employment, has a reasonable position to claim that they are not subject to U.S. income tax laws, since the individual's sole income would be from labor, representing a capitation tax, and a direct tax on property, that must be apportioned to be constitutional. Again, such income (wages from labor) falls outside of the powers granted Congress as a result of the 16th Amendment; and, Congress must comply with the limitations set forth in Article I, Section 9 requiring the apportionment rule.

In other words, the claim that wages are not taxable income may not be such a frivolous argument after all. However, to take this position in today's environment would most probably be quite costly; time consuming; and, one may have to rely on a jury, and an appeals court, or even the Supreme Court, to avoid incarceration.

And, even if such an individual prevailed criminally, chances are, the IRS would still pursue him or her civilly; and, he or she may still end up in financial ruin.

---

124 John E. Finn, Professor at Wesleyan University, *Civil Liberties and the Bill of Rights*, Part 1 of 3, 12 (2006). According to Professor Finn, monetary compensation for employment represents the "classic form of property." On page 93 he also quotes James Madison, "A man has a property in his opinions and the free communication of those opinions, and he also has a property in his religious opinions." He also said, "…the Founders had an individualistic conception of property… that they started from an assumption… that individual property rights would always trump any contrary community interest."

Furthermore, in addition to the limitations specifically identified (i.e. direct taxes must be apportioned and indirect taxes must be uniform), the administration and collection of all taxes must be in compliance with other provisions of the Constitution. Unfortunately, this appears to be a little known secret as far as the average American is concerned; and, obviously, has not been happening. In addition, the Courts have been complicit in this matter.[125] Accordingly, we seem to have "two constitutions, one for taxes and one for all other matters."[126]

Again, the 16th Amendment is not superior to and does not supersede any other provisions within the Constitution, including other amendments. Also, "[t]he Constitution is a law designed to restrict the lawmakers."[127] For as George Washington stated:

> The basis of our political systems is the right of the people to make and to alter their constitutions of government. But the constitution which at any time exists, till changed by an explicit and authentic act of the whole people, is sacredly obligatory upon all [including Congress, the IRS, and the Judiciary].[128]

> If in the opinion of the people the distribution or modification of the constitutional powers be in any particular wrong, let it be corrected by an amendment in the way which the Constitution designates, but let there be no change by usurpation; for though this in one instance may be the instrument of good; it is the customary weapon by which free governments are destroyed.[129]

---

125 Barnett, supra note 55, at 1-2.

126 Mazza, supra note 4.

127 Barnett, supra note 55, at 103.

128 George Washington, Quotations of George Washington (1732-1799), by Applewood Books, Inc., 13 (2003).

129 *Id.* at 24.

In addition, we should all remember these words as we go about our daily lives: "Government is not reason; it is not eloquence; it is force! Like fire, it is a dangerous servant and a fearful master."[130]

And finally, although Congress has the ability to tax just about anything, it must comply with the limitations set forth in the Constitution. Most everyone, who has any knowledge of tax issues, agrees that direct taxes must be apportioned; and, indirect taxes must be uniform.[131] But, not everyone agrees as to what is considered a direct tax; and, most seem to be confused as to how the 16th Amendment comes into play. The purpose of this discussion so far is to clear up some of this confusion.

However, there is another restriction or limitation that seems to be overlooked, i.e. any tax imposed must be administered and collected within the boundaries set forth in the Constitution. For example, the 4th Amendment says that, for the most part, a person has a right to keep his private papers free from the prying eyes of government. Then, it would seem that any law requiring individuals to make their financial records available for inspection by the IRS just may be unconstitutional, unless entirely voluntary.

---

130 *Id.* at 29.

131 The uniformity clause has not been addressed in this thesis; and, this limitation is worthy of a separate inquiry on its own. At least one person believes "... the IRS has adopted a practice of applying different tax laws to different states. This occurs when the IRS issues a formal opinion declaring that it will not enforce certain provisions of the Internal Revenue Code in states located within certain federal circuits." Accordingly, the IRS is violating the uniformity requirement set forth in Article I, Section 8. See Jeffrey S. Kinsler, *Circuit-Specific Application of the Internal Revenue Code: An Unconstitutional Tax*, 81 Denv. U.L. Rev. 113 (2003).

VII. FOURTH AND FIFTH AMENDMENT CONFLICTS

A. Fourth Amendment Issues

1. IRS versus the Cato Institute

According to the IRS, one of the frivolous arguments used by Tax protestors is the claim that filing a tax return violates the Fourth Amendment right to privacy; and, such an argument is false. Furthermore, no one has a right to disobey the law.[132] However, in their 61-page discussion under "Constitutional Amendment Claims," there is no mention of the Fourth Amendment and "Relevant Case Law."[133]

Furthermore, during testimony before a Congressional Committee, Stephen Moore, from the Cato Institute, stated, "I favor a national sales tax because I believe that the income tax is incompatible with a free society."[134] Additionally, the Cato Institute identified "10 areas of civil liberties abuse" that could be reduced or eliminated with the replacement of the income tax. Included among these abuses are references to violations

---

132 See supra note 1.
133 See supra note 99, at 24-31.
134 Stephen Moore, then Director of Fiscal Policy Studies for The Cato Institute, Testimony before the House Ways and Means Committee on *Replacing the Federal Income Tax*, Jun. 8, 1995, http://www.cato.org/testimony/ct-it68.html.

of the Fourth and Fifth Amendments.[135] According to the Cato Institute:

> In most situations, the Fourth Amendment guarantees that, before the government can search private property and seize records, it must demonstrate to a court that there is "probable cause" to believe that lawless conduct exists. However, the IRS's summons authority under tax code section 7602 allows it to obtain records of every description from any person without showing probable cause and without a court order. There has also been an explosion in information reporting required by the IRS and a big expansion in its computer searching for personal records. Recently, the IRS won the power to access financial data on Visa cards issued by foreign banks. Many examples of abusive IRS searches and seizures were revealed in U.S. Senate hearings in 1997.[136]

The Fourth Amendment states, "The right of the people to be secure in their persons, houses, papers, and effects, against unreasonable searches and seizures, shall not be violated, and no Warrants shall issue, but upon probable cause, supported by Oath or affirmation, and particularly describing the place to be searched, and the persons or things to be seized."[137] Based on a literal reading of this Amendment, the Cato Institute's position

---

135 Chris Edwards, Director of Fiscal Policy Studies for The Cato Institute, *Top Ten Civil Liberties Abuses of the Income Tax*, Apr. 2002, http://www.cato.org/pubs/tbb/tbb-0204-2.html. The civil liberties abuses identified are: (1) Vertical Inequality; (2) Horizontal Inequality; (3) Complexity, Ambiguity, and Uncertainty; (4) Huge Size and Instability of Tax Law; (5) Lack of Financial Privacy; (6) Denial of Due Process (Fifth Amendment); (7) Shifting of the Burden of Proof; (8) No Trial by Jury in Tax Court; (9) Unreasonable Searches and Seizures (Fourth Amendment); and, (10) Forced Self-Incrimination.

136 *Id.*

137 U.S. Const. amend. IV.

appears correct; and, if you look at the historical context behind this Amendment, one can easily see that a conflict exists between it and the administration of the individual income tax.

2. History and the Boyd Case

Accordingly, as stated by Charles Adams, the American Revolution "was probably more the consequence of the oppressive administration of taxes than the taxes themselves." For example, customs officers were provided with a writ of assistance allowing them to search for smuggled property. "The writ of assistance is important in American history because the threat of its use caused the founding fathers to place the Fourth Amendment in the Bill of Rights."[138]

Therefore, the purpose of this Amendment was "to restrain revenue agents; and, most of all, that tax agents cannot snoop without a court order based on an affidavit establishing probable cause."[139]

Following this rationale, in 1886, the Supreme Court decided that requiring a taxpayer to produce an invoice was a violation of his Fourth and Fifth Amendment rights; and, that the law that authorized the order was unconstitutional and void.[140] In *Boyd*, Justice Bradley said, "It is our opinion... that a compulsory production of a man's private papers to establish a criminal charge against him, or to forfeit his property, is within the scope of the Fourth Amendment to the Constitution..."[141] And,

> The principles laid down in this opinion affect the very essence of constitutional liberty and security... [T]hey

---

138 Adams, supra note 27, at 296.
139 *Id.*
140 Boyd v. U.S., 116 U.S. 616 (1886).
141 *Id.* at 528.

apply to all invasions on the part of the government and its employees of the sanctity of a man's home and the privacies of life. It is not the breaking of his doors, and the rummaging of his drawers, that constitutes the essence of the offence; but it is the invasion of his indefeasible right of personal security, personal liberty and private property, where the right has never been forfeited by his conviction of some public offence... [And,] ... any forcible and compulsory extortion of a man's own testimony or of his private papers to be used as evidence to convict him of crime or to forfeit his goods is within the condemnation of that judgment. In this regard the Fourth and Fifth Amendments run almost into each other.[142]

As indicated above, a law authorizing the compulsory production of private financial papers was deemed unconstitutional and void back in 1886. What has happened since then? The Fourth Amendment is still around. However, the Sixteenth Amendment was adopted subsequent to this ruling. But, as stated previously, the Sixteenth Amendment did not amend the Fourth Amendment, nor is it superior to it.

3. Boyd Ignored In Spite of Olmstead

However, today, by filing a Form 1040, U.S. Individual Income Tax Return, an individual is required to provide a summary of all financial transactions for the past year, along with an identification number, street address, phone number, and occupation. For the return to be accepted and deemed complete, the return must be signed "under penalties of perjury."[143] Then, on a random basis, if selected for an audit, it is expected that the taxpayer provide

---

142 *Id.* at 630.
143 Form 1040 (2006), bottom of page 2, Sign Here.

complete details to support every item listed on the tax return filed.

Furthermore, if a person fails to provide all the necessary information, as determined solely by the IRS, and claims that filing a tax return is "an unreasonable search and seizure contrary to the Fourth Amendment," a penalty of $5,000 may be immediately assessed.[144] In addition, a simple mistake or omission of an item of income may result in substantial civil penalties with a threat of criminal prosecution.

But, common sense would suggest that if the Fourth Amendment is suppose to mean something, the individual income tax laws, as they are administered today, should be deemed unconstitutional and void based on the Supreme Court decision in *Boyd*. Furthermore, in a dissenting opinion delivered in 1928, Justice Brandeis said:

> The protection guaranteed by the Amendments [4th and 5th] is much broader in scope. The makers of our Constitution undertook to secure conditions favorable to the pursuit of happiness. They recognized the significance of man's spiritual nature, of his feelings and of his intellect. They knew that only a part of the pain, pleasure and satisfactions of life are to be found in material things. They sought to protect Americans in their beliefs, their thoughts, their emotions and their sensations. They conferred, as against the Government, the right to be let alone—the most comprehensive of rights and the right most valued by civilized men. To protect that right, every unjustifiable intrusion by the Government upon the privacy of the individual, whatever the means employed [e.g., passing

---

144 I.R.S. Notice 2007-30, 2007-14 I.R.B., http://www.irs.gov/pub/irs-drop/n-07-30.pdf.

laws requiring disclosure of all financial transactions], must be deemed a violation of the Fourth Amendment. And the use, as evidence in a criminal proceeding, of facts ascertained by such intrusion must be deemed a violation of the Fifth.[145]

"Every unjustifiable intrusion by the Government upon the privacy of the individual [i.e. passing laws requiring full disclosure of all financial transactions relating to the individual income tax] [should] be deemed a violation of the Fourth Amendment." According to *Boyd*, it was.

However, in a case in 1999, the Fifth Circuit stated, "... we have rejected as 'without merit' the contention that requiring the filing of a tax return violates the Fourth Amendment"; and, they cited *Flint*.[146] In a somewhat earlier tax protestor action, the Fifth Circuit stated, "This Court has already rejected similar frivolous claims, and repetition of this analysis is unnecessary... The ... fourth amendment claim is similarly without merit."[147]

In both the tax protestor cases mentioned above, the Fourth Amendment claim was deemed frivolous and the Fifth Circuit did not explain why... no reason or rationale and really no appropriate authority was cited for their position.

In one of the cases, they cited *Flint*. In *Flint*, Justice Day made the following statement: "Certainly the Amendment [Fourth] was not intended to prevent the ordinary procedure in use in many, perhaps most, of the States of requiring tax returns to be made, often under oath."[148]

---

145 Olmstead v. U.S., 277 U.S. 438, 479 (1928).
146 Boozer v. Commissioner, 84 A.F.T.R.2d (RIA) 6008, 3 (5th Cir. 1999).
147 Hallowell v. Commissioner, 54 A.F.T.R.2d (RIA) 6149, 6 (5th Cir. 1984).
148 See supra note 39, at 175.

However, it should be remembered that, in *Flint*, the Court was dealing with a corporate income tax that they ruled an excise tax for the privilege of doing business in corporate form. Since a corporation is a creation of the legislature, the same protections afforded an individual under the Constitution may not be available to this created entity.

Also, including *Flint*, these cases give absolutely no meaningful reason or rationale for their decisions; and, the ruling in *Boyd* is just ignored. Even though it was applicable; and, should have been dealt with in all three cases, especially by the Supreme Court in *Flint*. Otherwise, the Courts' actions are similar to a parent telling his or her child to do something. The child asks why—the response—because I said so. Is this really good law?

And, whatever happened to the principle of stare decisis—it appears the Courts, in this situation at least, used it selectively to justify their intended outcome, whether or not in "perpetuation of injustice."[149]

4. Another Look at History

In addition, it should be remembered that the Fourth Amendment was directly the result of colonial experience, with "a rich English experience to draw on." The phrase, "every man's house is his castle" was an extremely important maxim in England. Probably one of the more famous cases in England, in 1705, was Entick v. Carrington (19 Howell's State Trials 1029, 95 807). Pursuant

---

149 Stare decisis is Latin which means "to stand by things that have been settled: the doctrine under which courts adhere to precedents on questions of law in order to insure certainty, consistency, and stability in the administration of justice with departure from precedent permitted for compelling reasons (as to prevent the perpetuation of injustice)." See Merriam-Webster's Dictionary of Law, 467 (1996), special edition 2005.

to general warrants, officers of the state raided many homes in search of seditious materials attacking the King and government polices.[150]

Entick brought legal action because the state officers had broken into his home, broken into locked desk and boxes; and, among other things, seized printed charts and pamphlets. In an opinion, delivered by Lord Camden, the Court determined that the warrant and the behavior of state officers represented subversive action; and, was detrimental to 'all the comforts of society.' Furthermore, the issuance of a warrant for the seizure of all of a person's papers was 'contrary to the genius of the law of England.' In addition, the Court said the warrant was bad because it was not issued on a showing of probable cause; and, no record was required to be made of what had been seized.[151]

"In the colonies, smuggling rather than seditious libel afforded the leading examples of the necessity for protection against unreasonable searches and seizures. In order to enforce the revenue laws, English authorities made use of writs of assistance [discussed supra]."[152]

And therefore, "[t]he writ of assistance… caused the founding fathers to place the Fourth Amendment in the Bill of Rights."[153]

5. Back to the Boyd Case

Because of what happened in England and the colonies; and, as a result of the Bill of Rights, Congress understood that sending agents

---

150 CRS Annotated Constitution, *Fourth Amendment Search and Seizure; History*, http://www.law.cornell.edu/anncon/html/amdt4frag1_user.html.
151 *Id.*
152 *Id.*
153 Adams, supra note 27, at 296.

out on a 'fishing expedition' to search and seize property under the tax laws was a direct violation of the Fourth Amendment.

However, on June 22, 1874, Congress apparently thought they could avoid the limitations set forth in the Fourth Amendment; and, they passed an Act, which included a section requiring the production of "private books, invoices and papers, or else the allegations of the government attorney [would] be taken as confessed."[154] Unfortunately for Congress, in 1886 Justice Bradley saw through their efforts to skirt the Fourth Amendment.

In *Boyd*, the charge related to the importation of twenty-nine cases of glass, which was subject to the payment of duties; and, it became necessary to determine the quantity and value of the glass in order to prove the alleged fraud. The claimants were required by a court order to produce an invoice, which they did. But, "in a suit for forfeiture," they objected to the production of the invoice; and, "also that the statute, so far as it compels production of evidence to be used against [them], is unconstitutional and void." However, a jury ruled in favor of the government, which was affirmed by the Circuit Court.[155]

When the case arrived at the Supreme Court, Justice Bradley stated that the issues involved represented "a very grave question of constitutional law, involving the personal security, and privileges and immunities of the citizen."[156] Furthermore, that the requirement to produce books and records, although not demanded, was necessary in order to avoid the allegations to be taken as confessed, was tantamount to compelling their production.[157]

According to Justice Bradley:

---

154 See supra note 140, at Head notes by Justice Bradley 1.
155 See supra note 140, at 618, 747 and 526.
156 See supra note 140, at 526-619.
157 See supra note 140, at 622.

It is true that certain aggravating incidents of actual search and seizure, such as forcible entry into a man's house and searching amongst his papers, are wanting, and to this extent the proceeding under the act of 1874 is a mitigation of that which was authorized by former acts; but it accomplishes the substantial object of those acts in forcing from a party evidence against himself.[158]

It is our opinion, therefore, that a compulsory production of a man's private papers to establish a criminal charge against him, or to forfeit his property, is within the scope of the Fourth Amendment to the Constitution, in all cases in which a search and seizure would be; because it is a material ingredient, and effects the sole object and purpose of search and seizure.[159]

Therefore, the government is not entitled to a "man's private books and papers for the purpose of obtaining information therein contained, or of using them as evidence against him."[160]

As alluded to above, *Boyd* stands for the principle that Congress may tax just about anything, but, the administration and collection must be done within the limits set forth in the Constitution. Unfortunately, both Congress and the IRS are ignoring the principle established in *Boyd*.

"Justice Bradley died in harness in 1892... But he had foreseen the constitutional backsliding that was sure to come, and he built the rebuttal into *Boyd*:"[161]

---

158 *Id.*

159 See supra note 140, at 528.

160 See supra note 140, at 623.

161 Milton Hirsch and David O. Markus, *Column: Fourth Amendment Forum*, 26 Champion 57, Conclusion (July 2002).

It may be that it is the obnoxious thing in its mildest and least repulsive form; but illegitimate and unconstitutional practices get their first footing in that way, namely, by silent approaches and slight deviations from legal modes of procedure. This can only be obviated by adhering to the rule that constitutional provisions for the security of person and property should be liberally construed. A close and literal construction deprives them of half their efficacy, and leads to gradual depreciation of the right, as if it consisted more in sound than in substance. It is the duty of courts to be watchful for the constitutional rights of the citizen, and against any stealthy encroachments therein.[162]

6. Boyd is still Good Law

The last time I perused a Shepard's Summary for *Boyd*, it listed 4,352 citations. The case was followed 55 times; criticized 12 times; distinguished 82 times; not followed twice; questioned 36 times; and, overruled just once.

The case identified as over-ruling *Boyd* involved a conviction of a person for larceny of military property and false swearing at Fort Hood, Texas. It appears that a proper warrant was obtained to search for and confiscate stolen night vision goggles.[163] Although this case did not over-rule *Boyd*, the Court stated:

> ...the Supreme Court held that 'mere evidence,' as well as contraband and proceeds of a crime, could be seized pursuant to a valid warrant. *Hayden* thus negated the assumption in [*Boyd*], that papers could not be lawfully seized... The concerns of an evidentiary search were not

---

162 See supra note 140, at 535.
163 United States v. Light, 48 M.J. 187, C.A.A.F. (1998).

present in this case because the officers were seeking stolen property, specifically, stolen night-vision goggles.[164]

Why the Court made the statement about *Boyd* makes very little sense. In fact, *Boyd* actually supports the decision in this case, as explained by Justice Bradley:

> The search for and seizure of stolen or forfeited goods [e.g.. night vision goggles], or goods liable to duties and concealed to avoid payment thereof, are totally different things from a search for and seizure of a man's private books and papers for the purpose of obtaining information therein contained, or of using them as evidence against him... In the one case, the government is entitled to the possession of the property [stolen goods, e.g., night vision goggles]; in the other [private papers] it is not.[165]

As indicated in the discussion by Justice Bradley, under the doctrine of stare decisis, the Court should have cited *Boyd* as one of its authorities in support of its decision, rather than demean the case; and, therefore, suggesting that it should no longer be relied upon as good law.

Hayden is another example of the Supreme Court's effort to discredit *Boyd*; and, re-write the Constitution by changing the original meaning of certain words and terms. The majority opinion was delivered by Justice Brennan who stated, among other things: "We have recognized that the principal object of the Fourth Amendment is the protection of privacy rather than property, and have increasingly discarded fictional and procedural barriers rested on property concepts... This shift in emphasis from property to privacy has come about through a

164 *Id.* at 9.
165 See supra note 140, at 623.

subtle interplay of substantive and procedural reform."[166] This is exactly what Justice Bradley foretold would happen.

Furthermore, Justice Brennan appears to have admitted that he does not like the original expansive definition of property as understood by our Founders; and, built into our Constitution. This expansive definition of property was understood and explained quite well by Justice Bradley in *Boyd*.

However, even though Justice Fortas' issued a concurring opinion with Justice Brennan, he could not entirely agree as stated below:

> While I agree that the Fourth Amendment should not be held to require exclusion from evidence of the clothing as well as the weapons and ammunition found by the officers during the search [after a hot pursuit], I cannot join in the majority's broad—and in my judgment, totally unnecessary—repudiation of the so-called 'mere evidence' rule.[167]

In addition, according to Justice Douglas, in his dissenting opinion, the Fourth Amendment guarantee had, until the ruling in *Hayden*, two faces of privacy:

> (1) One creates a zone of privacy that may not be invaded by the police through raids, by legislators through laws, or by magistrates through the issuance of warrants.

> (2) A second creates a zone of privacy that may be invaded either by the police in hot pursuit or by a search incident to arrest or by a warrant issued by a magistrate on a showing of probable cause.[168]

---

166 Hayden v. U.S., 387 U.S. 294, 1649 (1967).

167 *Id*. at 1652-311.

168 *Id*. at 313.

Furthermore, "[t]he full privacy protected by the Fourth Amendment is... reached when we come to books, pamphlets, papers, letters, documents, and other personal effects. Unless they are contraband or instruments of the crime, they may not be reached by any warrant..."[169]

And finally, in his concluding remarks, Justice Douglas states:

> The constitutional philosophy, I think, clear. The personal effects and possessions of the individual (all contraband and the like excepted) are sacrosanct from prying eyes, from the long arm of the law, from any rummaging by police. Privacy involves the choice of the individual to disclose or to reveal what he believes, what he thinks, what he possesses. The article may be a nondescript work of art, a manuscript of a book, a personal account book, a diary, invoices, personal clothing, jewelry, or whatnot.

> Those who wrote the Bill of Rights believed that every individual needs both to communicate with others and to keep his affairs to himself. That dual aspect of privacy means that the individual should have the freedom to select for himself the time and circumstances when he will share his secrets with others and decide the extent of that sharing. This is his prerogative not the States'. The Framers, who were as knowledgeable as we, knew what police surveillance meant and how the practice of rummaging through one's personal effects could destroy freedom.[170]

As indicated above, it is extremely difficult to erase entirely good law—although many have tried and continue to do so. Therefore, in my opinion, the Cato Institute is correct in asserting that the

---

169 *Id.* at 321.
170 *Id.* at 323-324, 1659.

IRS's summons authority and its' "fishing expeditions" to locate unreported income, by searching financial and credit card records through third parties, is a violation of the Fourth Amendment.

Furthermore, requiring an individual to provide a summary of his or her financial affairs on tax returns and then, on a random basis, expect the person to provide complete details and supporting documentation of their entire financial dealings is exactly what the *Boyd* case was all about. According to Justice Bradley:

> ...any compulsory discovery by extorting the party's oath, or compelling the production of his private books and papers to convict him of crime, or to forfeit his property, is contrary to the principles of a free government. It is abhorrent to the instincts of an Englishman; it is abhorrent to the instincts of an American. It may suit the purposes of despotic power; but it cannot abide the pure atmosphere of political liberty and personal freedom.[171]

Therefore, the U.S. individual income tax, as administered today, is in conflict with the original intent and purpose of the Fourth Amendment. In addition, the Fourth Amendment has not been modified or changed in accordance with Article V of the Constitution; and, *Boyd* has not been entirely over-ruled by subsequent Supreme Court cases.[172]

---

171 See supra note 140, at 632.

172 The purpose of this thesis is not to discuss Fourth Amendment jurisprudence—only to point out potential conflicts associated with this Amendment and the income tax laws today. For example, I have not discussed Justice Harlan's two-part test in Katz concerning the concept of "expectation of privacy". However, on the surface, this concept—"What a person knowingly exposes to the public... is not a subject of Fourth Amendment protection"—could represent a strong argument for not providing the information requested on a tax return. But apparently, the consequences, of the two-part test, are unclear. See supra note 150, at The Interest Protected.

Accordingly, the argument that the requirement to file an individual income tax return violates the Fourth Amendment right to privacy does not seem so frivolous after all.

B. Fifth Amendment and Self-Incrimination

1. The IRS Position

According to the IRS, the contention that Taxpayers do not have to file returns or provide financial information because of the Fifth Amendment privilege against self-incrimination is considered a frivolous argument; and, has no basis in law. To support their position, they cite one Supreme Court case; and, five Circuit Court cases. In addition, they have issued Revenue Ruling 2005-19, warning taxpayers of the consequences of attempting to argue this position.[173] Suspiciously missing is any reference to *Boyd* (discussed supra).

The following is the IRS statement on the Law concerning the filing of tax returns and the Fifth Amendment:

> There is no constitutional right to refuse to file an income tax return on the ground that it violates the Fifth Amendment privilege against self-incrimination. In *United States v. Sullivan*, 274 U.S. 259, 264 (1927), the U.S. Supreme Court stated that the taxpayer 'could not draw a conjurer's circle around the whole matter by his own declaration that to write any word upon the government blank would bring him into danger of the law.' The failure to comply with the filing and reporting requirements of the federal tax laws will not be excused based upon blanket

---

173 See supra note 99, at 26.

assertions of the constitutional privilege against compelled self-incrimination under the Fifth Amendment.[174]

Therefore, according to the IRS, the filing of an individual income tax return does not violate the Fifth Amendment right against self-incrimination; and, such an argument is false. Furthermore, no one has a right to disobey the law.[175] However, they do subtly indicate that a problem or conflict may exist, i.e. blanket assertions of the constitutional privilege will not be excused.

2. The Cato Institute's Opinion

The Cato Institute has a much more honest appraisal of the potential conflict between the Fifth Amendment and the requirement to file an income tax return:

> The requirement to file tax returns sworn to under penalty of perjury operates to invalidate the Fifth Amendment protection against self-incrimination. Citizens face a legal dilemma. On the one hand, refusing to file a return would expose a citizen to prosecution for failure to file.

> On the other hand, disclosing information sought in tax returns constitutes a waiver of Fifth Amendment protections. The IRS can and does release that information to federal, state, and local agencies for both tax and non-tax law enforcement purposes.[176]

According to the Fifth Amendment, "... nor shall [any person] be compelled in any criminal case to be a witness against himself, nor be deprived of ... [any] property, without due process of law;

---

174 *Id.*
175 See supra note 1, Frivolous Arguments.
176 See supra note 135.

nor shall private property be taken for public use without just compensation."[177]

After reading the Fifth Amendment, if the words are to mean what they actually say, it seems quite clear that passing a law to require full disclosure of one's entire financial affairs (e.g., income tax laws); then making that person sign, under penalties of perjury, that all the information provided is complete and correct; is setting that person up to be a "witness against himself" should any discrepancies actually exist; and/or, there is a difference of opinion as to the operation and application of the tax laws. And, according to Dr. Williams, "[t]he Constitution was not written for intellectual elites; it was understandable to a nation of mostly farmers at the time it was written."[178]

Therefore, it would certainly seem that the Cato position is correct; and, is much more truthful than the IRS is willing to let the average U.S. taxpayer believe.

3. The Opinion in Sullivan versus the Founders

But, according to the IRS, in *Sullivan*, the Supreme Court specifically stated that filing a tax return was required; and, that a person could not claim that doing so was a violation of their Fifth Amendment privileges. In *Sullivan*, Justice Holmes opinion was quite short; and, his decision is as follows:

> As the defendant's income was taxed, the statute of course required a return... In the decision that this was contrary to the Constitution we are of the opinion that the protection of the Fifth Amendment was pressed too far. If the form of return provided called for answers that

177 U.S. Const. amend. V.
178 Williams, supra note 48.

the defendant was privileged from making he could have raised the objection in the return, but could not on that account refuse to make any return at all. It would be an extreme if not an extravagant application of the Fifth Amendment to say that it authorized a man to refuse to state the amount of his income because it had been made in crime. But if the defendant desired to test that or any other point he should have tested it in the return so that it could be passed upon. He could not draw a conjurer's circle around the whole matter by his own declaration that to write any word upon the government blank would bring him into danger of the law.[179]

Let's think about Justice Holmes' statement that it would be "an extravagant application of the Fifth Amendment to say that it authorized a man to refuse to state the amount of his income because it had been made in crime." The only way this statement makes any sense is if a person was only required to state his total income, rather than itemize it; and, in addition, the person was not required to prove his income. Otherwise, any disclosure or lack thereof, results in providing potentially incriminating information against oneself; or, raising suspicion creating an investigation by one or more government agencies. In other words, especially today, preparing a tax return, as expected, and being subject to an audit of all such information provided, and some information that may not, runs head into the Fifth Amendment.

And, if we look at how the Founders felt about this, Justice Holmes interpretation does not appear accurate, i.e. to argue that the income tax laws run afoul of the Fifth Amendment is not "an extravagant application of the Fifth Amendment." Accordingly, as stated supra, the Founders were extremely aware of the great

---

179 U.S. v. Sullivan, 274 U.S. 259, at 1040, 264 and 608.

Scottish economist and philosopher, Adam Smith; and, many of them studied under other Scots, who studied with him. Furthermore, James Madison recommended that Adam Smith's, "The Wealth of Nations," be included in the congressional library.[180]

In his discussion of Capitation Taxes, Adam Smith made the following observations:

> The mild government of England, when it assessed the different ranks of people to the poll-tax, contented itself with what that assessment happened to produce; and, required no compensation for the loss which the state might sustain either by those who could not pay, or by those who would not pay (for there were many such), and who, by the indulgent execution of the law, were not forced to pay.[181]

Accordingly, at one point in time, England's capitation or poll-tax, which resulted in a direct tax "upon the wages of labor," was voluntary; and, the government did not enforce the payment of such taxes.[182]

Furthermore, according to Adam Smith, "In those corrupted governments where there is at least a general suspicion of much unnecessary expence, and great misapplication of the public revenue, the laws that guard it are little respected."[183] Sounds just a little like the United States today. Why else would the IRS publish a 61-page document entitled, "The Truth About Frivolous Arguments".[184]

180　Klieforth and Munro, supra note 70, 71 and 72.

181　Smith, supra note 73, at 998.

182　Smith, supra note 73, at 996-999.

183　Smith, supra note 73, at 1033.

184　See supra note 99.

In addition, Adam Smith believed that the smuggler (tax evader), "would have been, in every respect, an excellent citizen, had not the laws of his country made a crime which nature never meant to be so."[185] The Founders knew and understood where Adam Smith was coming from; and, did not want any tax levied that was inquisitorial. The Fifth Amendment, if taken for what it says, prevents an income tax as it is administered today.

4. Justice Holmes and the Progressive Movement

As far as Justice Holmes' opinion in *Sullivan* is concerned, it's important to understand just what his politics were at the time he rendered his decision. The reason for this was best explained by Thomas Jefferson; and, unfortunately, his warning went unheeded:

> To consider the judges as the ultimate arbiters of all constitutional questions [is] a very dangerous doctrine indeed, and one which would place us under the despotism of an oligarchy. Our judges are as honest as other men, and not more so. They have with others, the same passions for party, for power, and the privilege of their corps... and their power the more dangerous as they are in office for life... It has long, however, been my opinion, and I have never shrunk from its expression... that the germ of dissolution of our federal government is in the constitution of the federal judiciary; an irresponsible body... working like gravity by night and by day, gaining a little to-day and little to-morrow, and advancing its noiseless step like a thief, over the field of jurisdiction, until all shall be usurped from the States, and the government of all be consolidated into one. To this I am opposed; because,

---

185 Smith, *supra* note 73, at 1033.

when all government, domestic and foreign, in little as in great things, shall be drawn to Washington as the center of all power, it will render powerless the checks provided of one government or another, and will become as venal and oppressive as the government from which we separated.[186]

Justice Holmes served on the Supreme Court from 1902 to 1932; and, "was admired by the Progressives of his day who concurred in his narrow reading of 'due process.'" Furthermore, "[h]e regularly dissented when the Court invoked due process to strike down economic legislation." And finally, when he died, he left "his residuary estate to the United States government."[187]

According to Professor Epstein, the progressive movement "occupied center stage" during the period Justice Holmes served on the Supreme Court.[188] Furthermore,

[t]he Progressive view of social progress equated active government with good government. Predictably, their theory of good government generated a compatible constitutional theory. Thus, any constitutional doctrine that stood in the way of comprehensive reforms had to be rejected or circumvented... [Furthermore], they thought that ever greater inequalities of wealth justified overriding constitutional protected rights of liberty, property, and contract. In all of this, the 'public interest' was to rank supreme.[189]

---

186 Thomas Jefferson, Democracy, selected & arranged by Saul K. Padover, Ph.D., The Classics of Liberty Library, 98-99 (1994).

187 http://en.wikipedia.org/wiki/Oliver_Wendell_Holmes%2C_Jr.

188 Epstein, supra note 54.

189 Epstein, supra note 54, at 7-8.

In addition, the progressive movement was all about "the power of science and economics, employed by government, to lift up the economic and social position of the general population... they were influenced ... by... social initiatives in 19th-century Germany."[190] Therefore, Adam Smith's economic theories were dismissed as irrelevant; and, it was now thought that government should step in and regulate the economy.[191] According to Professor Epstein:

> Writing in 1917 about those developments and the need for modern 'living' law, Louis Brandeis expressed the new view well when he castigated traditional formalist judges for their blind adherence—in the face of new realities—to outmoded 18th-century conceptions of liberty.[192]

Louis Brandeis, of course, was an associate of Justice Holmes on the Supreme Court. Furthermore, rather than proposing that the Constitution be amended, as required under Article V, Justice Brandeis seems to have been suggesting that the Supreme Court re-interpret the Constitution, which they appear to have done.[193]

Therefore, in *Sullivan* (cited by the IRS), Justice Holmes does not address or refer to the *Boyd* case. However, it would certainly seem that the decision in *Boyd* concerns the Fifth Amendment; and, that Justice Holmes should have dealt with it. Maybe, the reason he did not refer to *Boyd* was due to his political beliefs? After all, Justice Holmes left his residuary estate to the United States government, which suggests strongly, that he believed in

---

190 Epstein, supra note 54, at 3.

191 See Epstein, supra note 54, at 3-4.

192 Epstein, supra note 54, at 4.

193 See Epstein, supra note 54 and Barnett, supra note 55.

the ideals of the Progressives. And, better to ignore *Boyd* than "muddied the waters".

5. Boyd Should Be Considered

According to Justice Bradley, in *Boyd*, discussed at length supra,

> ...any compulsory discovery by extorting the party's oath, or compelling the production of his private books and papers, to convict him of crime, or to forfeit his property, is contrary to the principles of a free government. It is abhorrent to the instincts of an Englishman; it is abhorrent to the instincts of an American. It may suit the purposes of despotic power; but it cannot abide the pure atmosphere of political liberty and personal freedom.[194]

This is exactly what is happening when individuals comply with the income tax laws today, i.e., we are required to produce our "private books and records" and our "oath" is being extorted by signing our tax returns under penalties of perjury. Accordingly, as Justice Bradley so stated, "it is abhorrent to the instincts of an American."

And, as far as the criminal nature is concerned, Justice Bradley said the following:

> ...we have to deal with an act which expressly excludes criminal proceedings from its operation (though embracing civil suits for penalties and forfeitures), and with an information not technically a criminal proceeding, and neither, therefore, within the literal terms of the Fifth Amendment to the Constitution any more than it is

194 See supra note 140, at 632.

within the literal terms of the Fourth. Does this relieve the proceedings or the law from being obnoxious to the prohibitions of either? We think not; we think they are within the spirit of both.[195]

Consequently, in accordance with the precedent set in *Boyd*, Congress cannot pass a law to circumvent the Fifth Amendment; that is, it is the substance and not the form that counts. Therefore, since the section of the law requiring an individual to produce his books and records and extorts his oath, violates the spirit of the Fourth and Fifth Amendments, it is "obnoxious" to the Constitution; and, accordingly, should be null and void. The same should hold true today, as the income tax laws violate the spirit of both the Fourth and Fifth Amendments to the Constitution.

Justice Bradley further stated:

We have already noticed the intimate relation between the two amendments. They throw great light on each other. For the 'unreasonable searches and seizures' condemned in the Fourth Amendment are almost always made for the purpose of compelling a man to give evidence against himself, which in criminal cases is condemned in the Fifth Amendment; and compelling a man 'in a criminal case to be a witness against himself,' which is condemned in the Fifth Amendment, throws light on the question as to what is an 'unreasonable search and seizure' within the meaning of the Fourth Amendment.

And we have been unable to perceive that the seizure of a man's private books and papers to be used in evidence against him is substantially different from compelling him to be a witness against himself. We think it is within

---

195 See supra note 140, at 534.

the clear intent and meaning of those terms. We are also clearly of opinion that proceedings instituted for the purpose of declaring the forfeiture of a man's property by reasons of offences committed by him, though they may be civil in form, are in their nature criminal.[196]

Furthermore, according to Justice Bradley, in order to provide for the security and property of the individual, constitutional provisions should be liberally construed in favor of the individual. In addition, "It is the duty of the courts to be watchful for the constitutional rights of the citizen, and against any stealthy encroachments therein."[197]

Therefore, in accordance with *Boyd*, the individual income tax laws, as administered today, are certainly in conflict with the Fifth Amendment; and, if Justice Bradley were alive, I am certain he would find the income tax laws obnoxious to the Constitution ruling them null and void.

6.   Besides Boyd there is Garner

Not only did the IRS ignore the precedent established in *Boyd*, they failed to mention a more recent Supreme Court case that took place in 1976. In *Garner* the government provided as evidence copies of tax returns filed by Roy Garner from 1965 through 1967. On the tax returns he listed his occupation as 'professional gambler' and reported substantial income from 'the business of wagering and gambling'. The prosecution used his tax returns to "rebut his claim that his relationships with the other conspirators were innocent ones." Roy Garner was found guilty in a jury trial; and, on appeal to the 9th Circuit, the Court of Appeals "held that

---

196 See supra note 140, at 634.
197 See supra note 140, at 535.

Garner's failure to assert the privilege on his returns defeated his Fifth Amendment claim."[198]

In *Garner*, the Supreme Court stated that an individual "may rightfully refuse to answer unless and until he is protected at least against the use of his compelled answers and evidence derived therefrom in any subsequent criminal case in which he is a defendant." Furthermore, if he is not protected, the evidence cannot be used against him.[199]

Roy Garner claimed that if he had exercised his Fifth Amendment privilege on his tax return, he would have faced the possibility of criminal prosecution for failure to file; and, therefore argued "that the possibility of prosecution... compels a taxpayer to make incriminating disclosures rather than claim the privilege." The Supreme Court stated, "This contention is not entirely without force, but we find it unpersuasive."[200]

According to Justice Marshall, "I agree with the Court that petitioner [Roy Garner], having made incriminating disclosures on his income tax returns rather than having claimed the privilege against self-incrimination, cannot thereafter assert the privilege to bar the introduction of his returns in a criminal prosecution."[201]

Furthermore, "the Court notes that only a 'willful' failure to make a return is punishable under § 7203, and that 'a defendant could not properly be convicted for an erroneous claim of privilege asserted in good faith'."[202]

---

198 Garner v. U.S., 424 U.S. 648, 650 & 375 (1976).
199 *Id.* at 1182.
200 *Id.* at 662.
201 *Id.* at 385.
202 *Id.*

Accordingly, an individual's income tax returns can be used against him or her in a criminal prosecution by the IRS; and, just about any other government agency. To avoid this possibility, one must claim his or her right against self-incrimination, under the Fifth Amendment, before actually filing a tax return. This is done by either not disclosing the incriminating information in your return or by not filing a return at all.

In *Garner*, they not only used his stated occupation against him, they also used his substantial income reported in his returns. Therefore, an individual may not even realize what information provided in a tax return may be able to be used against him or her at the time of actually filing a return.

Consequently, by filing a tax return an individual is deemed to have waived his Fifth Amendment rights. The proverbial Catch-22: To preserve these rights, by not filing, will most probably result in prosecution under Section 7203 for failure to file a return. However, as stated by Justice Marshall, and after much wasted time and money, you would have "a valid claim of privilege" as a defense against such a prosecution.

As indicated above, the IRS and the forms and instructions that accompany the individual income tax returns do not inform the U.S. citizen or resident that by filing a tax return, you are waiving your Fifth Amendment privilege against self-incrimination. "This [represents] a fraud on the public."[203]

Accordingly, the income tax laws, as applied to the individual today, conflict with the Fifth Amendment; and, therefore, are incompatible with a free society.

---

203 See Barnett, supra note 55, at 2.

VIII. THE SLAVE TAX

Dr. Alan Keyes has stated, "… we must abolish the income tax and replace it with the tax system that was intended by our founders when this nation began—a tax system that leaves our people in control of 100 percent of their dollars… The income tax is a slave tax—inherently incompatible with freedom."[204] Continuing with this reasoning, Dr. Keyes says, "We ought to have realized that the income tax is utterly incompatible with liberty—it is actually a form of slavery."[205] Furthermore, "[the] income tax usurps privacy, allows the federal government to control income and paves a path to tyranny."[206]

According to the Thirteenth Amendment, Section 1: "Neither slavery nor involuntary servitude, except as punishment for a crime whereof the party shall have been duly convicted, shall

---

204 Alan Keyes, *Bushwhacking Taxes*, Jan. 20, 2001, http://www.worldnetdaily.com/news/article.asp?ARTICLE_ID=21422.

205 Alan Keyes, *The End of Income Tax, The Return of Economic Liberty*, Aug. 19, 2002, http://www.renewamerica.us/archives/print.php?file=%2Farchives%2Fcolumns%2F02_08… Dr. Keyes also explained that our Founders wanted to "…avoid this path to tyranny… So they made a direct tax on the income of individuals unconstitutional." This is incorrect because a direct tax was not unconstitutional per se… only if it was not apportioned. The Founders made it extremely difficult to levy a tax on incomes, if the income was considered a direct tax, because of this apportionment requirement. Unfortunately, as a result of this misstatement, Dr. Keyes loses some his credibility; and, his entire message may be disregarded by many.

206 Alan Keyes, *The Injustice of Income Tax*, Jun. 22, 2002, http://www.apfn.net/Doc-100_bankruptcy39.htm.

exist within the United States, or any place subject to their jurisdiction."[207]

The question becomes... when does slavery or involuntary servitude begin as it relates to the federal government? As a former auditor, I was taught that once an item of income or expense became material, then something had to be done about it; and, materiality was defined as 10% or greater. Therefore, if the federal government takes 10% or more of an individual's income, it may be in violation of the 13th Amendment.

As of this date, the maximum tax rate is 35% for individuals. So, for certain taxpayers, the first 35% of every dollar earned goes first to the United States Treasury, with the remainder to the employee. Therefore, it would certainly appear that Dr. Keyes may have a valid point, i.e. the income tax is a slave tax.

However, the IRS has taken the position that anyone who claims that the income tax laws violate the Thirteenth Amendment is making a frivolous argument. Here's their position:

> The Thirteenth Amendment to the United States Constitution prohibits slavery within the United States, as well as the imposition of involuntary servitude, except as punishment for a crime of which a person shall have been duly convicted. In *Porth v. Brodrick*, 214 F.2d 925, 926 (10th Cir. 1954), the Court of Appeals stated that 'if the requirements of the tax laws were to be classed as servitude, they would not be the kind of involuntary servitude referred to in the Thirteenth Amendment.' Courts have consistently found arguments that taxation constitutes a form of involuntary servitude to be frivolous.[208]

---

207 U.S. Const. amend. XIII.
208 See supra note 99, at 27.

The opinion cited by the IRS is very short but, can be summed up by the Court as follows:

> The allegations of the petition are very broad and it is difficult, if not impossible, to determine therefrom just what the complaint is except that there exists a strong dislike for the taxing procedure.
>
> [Furthermore], if the requirements of the tax laws were to be classed as servitude, they would not be the kind of involuntary servitude referred to in the Thirteenth Amendment.[209]

As indicated above, the 10th Circuit gave no reasoning for their decision other than demonstrating their belief that the federal taxing powers are unlimited; and, apparently, the 13th Amendment only applies to other individuals and the States, not the federal government.

In 1973, the President of the American Institute of Certified Public Accountants, Walter E. Olsen, in an article for the Wall Street Journal mocking the U.S. income tax system, wrote about the debates held in Congress concerning the first income tax passed after the ratification of the 16th Amendment:

> A fear expressed by a number of opponents was that the proposed law, with its low rates was the camel's nose under the tent that once a tax on incomes was enacted, rates would tend to rise. Senator William E. Borah of Idaho was outraged by such anxieties, and derided a suggestion that the rate might eventually climb as high as 20 percent. Who, he asked, could impose such socialistic, confiscatory rates? Only Congress. And how could

---

209 Porth v. Brodrick, 214 F.2d 925, 3 (10th Cir. 1954).

Congress, the Representatives of the American People, be so lacking in fairness, justice and patriotism?[210]

Apparently, Senator Borah may have also believed that high tax rates, say 10%-to-20% or more, represented involuntary servitude, i.e. socialistic and confiscatory and lacking in fairness and justice.

In addition, in 1956 T. Coleman Andrews stated:

> As Commissioner of Internal Revenue I often thought how far we had gone toward consuming ourselves 'through excessive and unjust taxation.' We have failed to realize, it seems to me, that through our tax system we have been playing right into the hands of the Marxists, who gleefully hail the income tax as the one sure instrument that will bring capitalism to its knees.
>
> We have also failed utterly to see that Communism is not a political philosophy or plan but rather is a state of impotence to which those marked for subjugation by would-be dictators must be, and are, reduced in order to assure absence of effective resistance.
>
> But there are other reasons for taking a dim view of our tax system, particularly the income tax, that are no less urgent than the fact that the system has become an ideological bombshell. I shall confine my comments primarily to the income tax. That alone is such a monstrous evil that it is hardly necessary to deal with other categories.[211]

---

210 http://en.wikipedia.org/wiki/William_Borah.

211 T. Coleman Andrews, A Collection of His Writings, vol. 2, edited by Edward N. Coffman and Daniel L. Jensen, 477 (1996).

Accordingly, "excessive and unjust taxation" may also be categorized as involuntary servitude when referring to the income tax. Although there may not be an arguable legal position that the income tax laws violate the Thirteenth Amendment, high individual income tax rates do tend to violate the spirit of the Amendment; and generally, the overall purpose of the Constitution. Furthermore, you might ask yourself, at what effective tax rate does the income tax become confiscatory; and, subjects U.S. citizens and residents to involuntary servitude? My number is 10%, is yours 35%, 50% or 100%?

IX. CONCLUSION

A. Signs of a Bad Tax

Adam Smith, in "The Wealth of Nations," identified four signs of a bad tax system that, if any one of them existed, would ultimately destroy the wealth of a nation:[212]

First, a tax is bad if it requires a large bureaucracy with "a great number of officers, whose salaries may eat up the greater part of the produce of the tax, and whose perquisites may impose another additional tax on the people."[213]

Second, if a tax discourages investment or employment, by taking funds away from "the industry of the people," which could be invested to create more jobs, it is a bad tax.[214]

Third, a tax is bad if it encourages tax evasion because the penalties and forfeitures may ruin unsuccessful tax evaders; and therefore, put an end to the benefits the community receives "from the employment of their capital." According to Adam Smith:

> An injudicious tax offers a great temptation to smuggling [tax evasion]. But the penalties must rise in proportion to the temptation. The law, contrary to all the ordinary

---

212 Adams, supra note 5, at 216.
213 Smith, supra note 73, at 946-947.
214 *Id.*

principles of justice, first creates the temptation, and then punishes those who yield to it...[215]

Fourth, a tax is bad if it subjects "the people to the frequent visits and odious examination of the tax-gatherers" causing "unnecessary trouble, vexation, and oppression."[216]

Therefore, according to Adam Smith, if, just one of these four signs are present within a tax system, the "taxes are frequently so much more burdensome to the people than they are beneficial to the sovereign [government]."[217] Today, all four signs are present with respect to the income tax laws.

B. Founders Understood Bad Taxes

Our Founders were well aware of the four signs of bad taxes expressed by Adam Smith; and, using the ideas of the Scottish Enlightenment, they designed a system of limited government funded by low indirect taxes. They understood that taxation was "the root of most evil" and were determined not to repeat the mistakes of the Europeans.[218]

C. Direct and Indirect Taxes

The concept of direct and indirect taxes was easily understood by our Founders. Furthermore, "direct taxes were looked upon with the utmost disfavor. In Madison's words, they were for an 'extraordinary emergency'." This fear of direct taxation went "all the way back in history to the Greeks and the Romans, who

---

215 *Id.*

216 *Id.*

217 *Id.*

218 Adams, supra note 5.

taught that tyranny was the inevitable consequence of permanent, direct taxation."[219]

Accordingly, the Founders made sure that all direct taxes must be apportioned in accordance with the census, a concept not easy to comply with. As a result, and, as planned, direct taxation would not be used until an "extraordinary emergency" required such taxation.

The difference between direct taxes and indirect taxes was easily understood by our Founders; and, everyone else at the time our Constitution was written and adopted. Direct taxes were taxes raised on the capital or revenue of the people; and, indirect taxes were raised on their expense. Also, a tax was called direct when it was taken directly from property or labor.

In addition, many dictionaries at that time described an income tax "as a capitation tax imposed upon persons in consideration of the amount of their property and their profits."[220] Furthermore, our Founders believed that wages for labor represented property.

Therefore, for over 75 years the U.S. government survived using only indirect taxes (e.g., duties, imposts and excises). There was no income tax or other direct taxation during this period, with the exception of a tax on carriages resulting from Hamilton's successful argument, in *Hylton*, that a carriage tax was always deemed an indirect tax in England. Using this same argument, an income tax was always deemed a direct tax in England.

Again, these definitions and distinctions were readily understood by all until certain members of the legislature, aided by members of the judiciary having similar political motives, decided that the government needed more money; and, wanted to use direct

219 Adams, supra note 5, at 57.
220 See supra note 60.

taxation without the required limitation of apportionment spelled out in the Constitution.

As stated by Thomas Jefferson, "The natural progress of things is for liberty to yield and government to gain ground."[221]

However, even though these original meanings have been ignored and purposely forgotten, they are still the law; and, have only been modified to a limited degree by the Sixteenth Amendment.

D. Pollock, Flint and the Sixteenth Amendment

In 1895, Chief Justice Fuller and Justice Field, in *Pollock*, made great strides in forcing Congress to comply with the limitations set forth in the Constitution concerning the apportionment requirement for direct taxes. Chief Justice Fuller explained the original meaning of indirect and direct taxes as understood by our Founders:

> ... all taxes paid primarily by persons who can shift the burden upon someone else, or who are under no legal compulsion to pay them, are considered indirect taxes; but a tax upon property holders in respect of their estates, whether real or personal, or of the income yielded by such estates, and the payment of which cannot be avoided, are direct taxes.[222]

Also, Justice Field explained that income taxes were always considered direct taxes in the British Parliament; and, "There is no such thing in the theory of our national government as unlimited power of taxation in Congress."[223]

---

221 Jefferson, supra note 59, at 16.

222 See supra note 29, at 558.

223 See supra note 29, 589 & 826.

However, in *Pollock*, the entire income tax statute was ruled unconstitutional because a tax on real estate and personal property was considered a direct tax; and, therefore, the income from such property would also be a direct tax. Since all direct taxes are subject to the rule of apportionment, and apportionment was not required, the tax statute was ruled null and void.

So, for a period of approximately 15 years, there was no income tax. But, in 1909 Congress passed a corporate income tax, which, in *Flint*, was ruled an excise tax for the privilege of doing business in corporate form.

Then in 1913, the Sixteenth Amendment was ratified. The purpose of the Sixteenth Amendment was to over-rule the decision in *Pollock*; and, not to grant Congress any new taxing powers. In *Pollock*, if the source of the income was direct, then the income would also be direct, thereby subjecting an otherwise indirect tax (the income) to the rule of apportionment. Therefore, because of *Pollock*, if the source of the income was direct, then the income would also be considered direct. The Sixteenth Amendment over-ruled this decision. Congress no longer had to look to the source in determining whether or not the income was direct or indirect... the income stood on its own.

But, if the income is direct in the first place, i.e. wages of labor (property) or a capitation tax (imposed on persons in consideration of the amount of their property and profits), it is subject to the rule of apportionment for the tax to be constitutional.

This is not the prevailing view but, the prevailing view appears to conflict with the original intent of our Founders; and, if one looks deeply into the arguments used today, it is extremely difficult to reconcile them with our Constitution. More specifically, the prevailing view cannot be reconciled.

E. Boyd and the Fourth and Fifth Amendments

Again, the Sixteenth Amendment gave Congress no new taxing powers. It only over-ruled the decision in *Pollock*. It did not amend, modify, or replace any other provisions in the Constitution, in particular the Fourth and Fifth Amendments. Furthermore, it is not superior to any other amendments, including the limitations[224] on Congress' taxing powers in Article I, Sections 8 & 9; and, the protections afforded U.S. citizens and residents under the Fourth and Fifth Amendments.

In *Boyd*, Justice Bradley explained quite well the type of government our Founders established and the reasons that the Fourth and Fifth Amendments were included in our Constitution:

> …any compulsory discovery by extorting the party's oath, or compelling the production of his private books and papers to convict him of crime, or to forfeit his property, is contrary to the principles of a free government. It is abhorrent to the instincts of an Englishman; it is abhorrent to the instincts of an American. It may suit the purposes of despotic power; but it cannot abide the pure atmosphere of political liberty and personal freedom.[225]

If Justice Bradley were alive today, just as he did in 1886, the income tax laws, as administered today, would be considered repugnant to the Constitution, a direct violation of the Fourth and Fifth Amendments; and accordingly, ruled null and void.

The decision in *Boyd* is still pertinent today. It is good law; and, supports the original meaning and purposes of the Fourth and Fifth Amendments.

---

224 The limitations referred to include the rule of apportionment for all direct taxes and the uniformity rule for indirect taxes.

225 See supra note 140, at 632.

Even ignoring *Boyd*, the Supreme Court has specifically stated, in *Garner*, that an individual taxpayer has waived his Fifth Amendment privileges as it relates to the completion and actual filing of an individual income tax return.

The average U.S. taxpayer has no idea that, by filing an individual income tax return, he or she is waiving his or her Fifth Amendment privileges as it relates to all items disclosed in the return; and, the IRS says that such a position represents a frivolous argument.

If our government was being honest and above board, it might consider something similar to a "Miranda warning,"[226] to be included with the instructions accompanying Form 1040, U.S. Individual Income Tax Return.

Accordingly, *Boyd* says that the individual income tax, as administered today, should be null and void; and, *Garner* says, by filing an individual income tax return, one waives his or her rights against self-incrimination under the Fifth Amendment.

Therefore, the U.S. individual income tax is certainly incompatible with our rights as set forth in the Fourth and Fifth Amendments to the United States Constitution.

---

226 Miranda v. Arizona, 384 U.S. 436 (1966). In *Miranda*, "a defendant was required to be warned before questioning that he had the right to remain silent [e.g., right to not complete a tax return], and that anything he said [e.g., included in his tax return], can be used against him in a court of law. A defendant was required to be to told that he had the right to the presence of an attorney [e.g., that one should consult an attorney before filing a tax return], and if he cannot afford an attorney one was to be appointed for him prior to any questioning [e.g., prior to completing his tax return], if he so desired. After these warnings were given [e.g., included with tax return instructions and referenced boldly on the front of each page of the tax return], a defendant could knowingly and intelligently waive these rights and agree to answer questions or make a statement [e.g., make a tax return]."

F. Income Tax is Incompatible with a Free Society

There are other reasons why the U.S. individual income tax may be incompatible with a free society.[227] However, I have only addressed the problems associated with the definitions of direct and indirect taxes and the related limitations; the problems associated with the interpretation of the Sixteenth Amendment; and, the specific conflicts related to the administration of the individual income tax and the rights granted U.S. citizens and residents under the Fourth and Fifth Amendments.[228]

Furthermore, even though Congress has unlimited taxing power, it must comply with the limitations set forth in the Constitution. If Congress wants to continually redefine the meaning of incomes, it must do so by using the Amendment process established in Article V of the Constitution; and, not by passing legislation. If Congress wants to tax wages of labor and not be subject to the rule of apportionment, since a tax on the wages of labor is both property and a capitation tax, it must pass an excise tax applicable to specific occupations (e.g., law, medicine, engineering, government employees, etc.).

In addition, regardless of the taxes imposed by Congress, the administration and collection of the taxes must be done constitutionally. In other words, Congress cannot pass laws requiring U.S. citizens and residents to waive their rights under the Constitution, e.g., the Fourth and Fifth Amendments.

Unfortunately, today, the Congress, the IRS, and the Judiciary are violating the rights of all U.S. individuals when it comes to the individual income tax. This is a fraud on the public.[229]

---

227 See supra note 131 and 135.

228 The "due process" requirement included in the Fifth Amendment has not been addressed in this thesis; and, is worthy of consideration on its own.

229 See Barnett, supra note 55, at 2.

Before this fraud becomes more readily understood by the populace at large, it would be prudent for Congress to replace the U.S. individual income tax with a national sales tax or something similar; get rid of the "Gestapo Tactics" of the IRS in forcing people to waive their rights; and, start the amendment process in Article V to abolish the Sixteenth Amendment.

If Congress does not have the stomach to do the right thing, the Judiciary needs to step up and take a good hard look at some very bad precedents that make little sense; and, are contradictory to the spirit of the Constitution.

Unfortunately, every argument I have focused on in this discussion has been deemed a frivolous argument by both the IRS and the Judiciary. If the people cannot get a fair hearing in Court, because legal counsel is threatened with penalties and disbarment for proposing arguments that the Court dislikes,[230] I can certainly understand the meaning, purpose, and the need for the Second Amendment.[231] This may appear to be a flippant remark. But our history is filled with examples of bloody tax revolts.[232] It behooves us to do something about our tax system before it is too late.

And finally, I will close with a quote from Charles Adams which supports my thesis that the U.S. individual income tax is incompatible with a free society:

---

230 If the Courts continue to fine attorneys and dismiss arguments as being frivolous without a fair hearing, it would seem to me to be a possible "due process" issue; and maybe, a First Amendment issue... something to consider for a future thesis.

231 U.S. Const. amend II. "...the right of the people to keep and bear Arms, shall not be infringed."

232 Adams, supra note 5. The book is about the tax revolts that built America.

Our tax destructiveness is on all fronts and we appear to be following the course of many great nations of the past—we are taxing ourselves to death, and not just economically. We have violated the tax rules our forefathers warned us about...

The so-called virtues of our income tax system are as phony as the virtues of socialism.[233]

Dum spiro, spero—While I breath I hope.

Slainte mhath.

---

233 Adams, supra note 27, at 473.